HOUGHTON MIFFLIN COMPANY
EDITORIAL ADVISORY COMMITTEE IN EDUCATION

C. GILBERT WRENN
MACALESTER COLLEGE

VAN CLEVE MORRIS
UNIVERSITY OF ILLINOIS AT CHICAGO CIRCLE

SAMUEL A. KIRK
UNIVERSITY OF ILLINOIS

WILLIAM VAN TIL
INDIANA STATE UNIVERSITY

CHARLES S. BENSON
UNIVERSITY OF CALIFORNIA, BERKELEY

ROBERT H. ANDERSON
HARVARD UNIVERSITY

Study Guide to accompany

Psychology Applied to Teaching

Robert F. Biehler

Chico State College

Houghton Mifflin Company · Boston

New York · Atlanta · Geneva, Illinois · Dallas · Palo Alto

Copyright © 1971 by Houghton Mifflin Company.

All rights reserved. No part of this work may be reproduced or transmitted in any form or by any means, electronic or mechanical, including photocopying and recording, or by any information storage or retrieval system, without permission in writing from the publisher.

Printed in the U.S.A.

ISBN: 0–395–04193–7

Contents

Part Six / Individual Differences and Adjustment

Suggestions for Using
This Study Guide

This Study Guide has been prepared to supplement *Psychology Applied to Teaching*. The major goal of the text is to help you apply the principles of psychology to the art of teaching. You are asked to read, learn, and think about the subject matter of educational psychology on the assumption that you can thereby become better prepared to solve problems of pedagogy when you are a teacher.

To apply principles of psychology in a manner which will be consistent with your own personality, and to remain flexible and innovative in adjusting to different students and teaching situations, you will need to function intuitively. Some prospective teachers argue that too much concern for facts and theories may interfere with their natural abilities and inclinations. A different point of view has been expressed by Jerome Bruner (whose observations are noted at many places in the text). Bruner points out that "intuitive thinking rests on familiarity with the domain of knowledge involved and with its structure." By means of the Study Guide you should be able to master material presented in the text in such a way that you will become thoroughly familiar with the domain and structure of educational psychology and thus be *assisted* to teach intuitively and innovatively. In this sense mastery of information is an aid—rather than a hindrance—to your intuitive individuality.

A common complaint of contemporary education centers around dislike for a "memorize and regurgitate" approach to study. Perhaps you share this distaste for educational experiences which emphasize the ability to repeat what is said by an author or lecturer. The exercises for this Study Guide try to avoid such a "ritualistic" approach to learning by basing questions on the Key Points listed at the beginning of each chapter. It is hoped thus to reduce (to some extent anyway) mere repetition of information exactly as it appears in the text. The classification of Key Points is intended to let you interpret information in a different frame of reference from that presented in the chapter. This is seen to be an advantage in that you are given the opportunity to test your understanding of ideas by applying them and interpreting them in another context. It is also hoped that grasping the overall structure of ideas will allow you to fill in the gaps (so to speak) in terms of your own interests and inclinations. You should therefore have greater freedom to make your own personal interpretation of matters discussed as opposed to merely repeating what the text says.

While the use of Key Points is intended to permit a degree of freedom for you to interpret information presented in the text in your own way, you are nevertheless asked to demonstrate your awareness of what is covered in the text. One reason for asking you to do this is that you are more likely to grasp the significance and recognize the interrelationships of concepts, principles, and theories discussed if you are familiar with the details and structure of the presentation. To acquire such familiarity you will need to read the text with care. Another reason for asking you to record your interpretations of text material in this Study Guide is to encourage you to test yourself on whether you understand the Key Points clearly enough to explain and apply them. Merely repeating others' words is a rudimentary form of learning. Being able to state an idea in your own words, to apply it, to explain how it relates to other ideas, to comment on its possible significance to a teacher—these are more advanced and valuable kinds of learning, and the questions in this Study Guide aim to encourage such learning.

In making use of the questions derived from the Key Points for each chapter, you are urged to follow this procedure:

1. After reading a chapter, refer back to the list of Key Points printed at the start of the chapter. Ask yourself whether you have at least some awareness of what each point refers to. If you draw a blank for any points, underline them for future reference.

2. If you are to be tested on a given chapter, reread the material, paying special attention to the underlined points you were unable to explain after the first reading.

3. Write out answers to the questions in this Study Guide (without referring to the text).

4. Compare your answers to the appropriate sections of the text (which are identified by marginal notes in color) and evaluate them. If you feel you have not adequately answered a question, make notes in the Study Guide to include omissions or correct errors. (You might use a pen with ink of a different color to emphasize points that need extra attention later. If referral to the text is not sufficient, ask your instructor for assistance.)

5. When studying for exams, use the notes in the Study Guide as the basis for final review.

In addition to questions designed to help you master the text material, a series of supplementary readings and exercises for each chapter is included.

These suggestions bear on further reading, thinking, and writing in terms of your personal interests. Most of the assignments center around the exploration of books which discuss various points taken up in the text. This should permit you to gain deeper understanding of ideas briefly mentioned in the text discussion. Perhaps it also will get you into the habit of reading comprehensive and systematic analyses of issues in psychology and education.

The supplementary readings include titles from a variety of fields, not just those within the traditional subject areas of psychology. Only a few teachers are directly concerned with psychology (and are thus likely to read books in psychology), and, besides, it will be to your advantage to get away from the arbitrary and artificial division of knowledge into separate fields. Compartmentalization of ideas is often necessary in organizing a college curriculum but has the disadvantage of sometimes obscuring interrelationships between fields. It is possible, desirable, and potentially valuable to make "educational" or "psychological" interpretations of books written by humanists, natural scientists, or novelists, but in order to do this you may need to overcome the inclination to put men and their ideas into academic pigeonholes. If you begin to make interpretations which cross traditional subject-area lines by reading books other than regular psychology texts, perhaps you'll find this practice will persist after you graduate. And this in turn might get you into the habit of looking for ideas and observations from all kinds of sources which you may be able to use in understanding students and education and in improving your teaching.

An obvious difficulty about supplementary assignments is that you will scarcely have time to do a great deal of outside reading. Perhaps you have frequently felt pressured when asked to read and report on complete books. If you have higher-priority requirements such as study for other courses, exams to prepare for, term papers to write, or a part-time job, you may find it next to impossible to read an additional 400-page book. The suggestions for further reading included in this Study Guide, therefore, ask you to react in a brief way to selected *parts* of books. The aim is to have you at least *sample* a number of books without feeling unduly pressed. In the process you may not only discover books you will want to read more completely at your leisure but become aware of interesting new publications which can be of value when you are teaching.

(Note: Whenever possible, paperbacks have been recommended for further reading. Since they are usually relatively inexpensive, you might purchase copies of promising titles now and build up a library for careful reading and reference later on.)

As you will discover, numerous exercises for reading, thinking, and discussion are given for each chapter. The idea is to provide a wide enough choice so that almost any future teacher will find at least a few suggestions of personal relevance. The exercises have been written so that your instructor can base supplementary assignments on them. If you *are* asked to turn in one or more reports, you will probably read the entire series of exercises as you search for a topic of interest. If you are *not* asked to write any supplementary reports, you should at least peruse the lists of suggestions on your own for two reasons: First, simply reading and thinking about a particular exercise may clarify points made in the text. Even without responding to the suggestions in a formal way, you may still benefit from just thinking about them. Second, you may discover (or at least become aware of) ideas that will be of value once you begin to teach. At present you may have neither the inclination nor the opportunity to read a book, observe student behavior, or try a simple experiment with a group of pupils. But as a teacher encountering some of the complexities of pedagogy, you may find that suggestions which at this stage appear pointless, or impossible, have suddenly become highly relevant.

Part One / Background

1

Prologue

Key Points

Criteria

Bases for judging validity of research findings: observance of sufficient number of random cases, use of a control group, concise and objective observation, testing of all plausible hypotheses

Concepts

Specific transfer of skills, general transfer of principles, structure (Bruner)
Teacher-practitioner and teacher-theorist (Stephens)
Teaching as testing-of-hypothesis behavior (Coladarci)

Principles

Laying down by science of laws within which rules of art of teaching must fall; agreement of many diverse teaching methods with such laws (James)

Theories

Spontaneous schooling (Stephens)

Methodology

Theoretical-deductive, empirical-inductive modes of thought
Using methods of science to avoid wishful thinking, emotional involvement, and unsystematic theorizing

Chapter Contents

Testing and Organizing Your Knowledge of Key Points in Chapter 1

If you thoroughly understand the main themes discussed in Chapter 1 of the text, you should know at least something about each of the Key Points listed at the start of the chapter. If you have read the chapter carefully, informally tested your awareness of the significance of the Key Points, and reread the chapter with special attention to items you were vague about, you should be able to respond to the questions below. After recording your responses, refer back to the text to check on the completeness and accuracy of your answers and make any necessary corrections or additions so that you will have complete notes for future reference. To encourage you to think about the *significance* of the various ideas stressed, you are asked (when appropriate) not only to describe the term, concept, or theory but to comment on why and how it might be meaningful to you. In case you are unable to explain a given point to your own satisfaction even after referring to the text, compare your notes with those of a fellow student or ask your instructor for clarification.

Criteria

New developments in educational psychology—as well as reassessments of established procedures in education—are based on research. In order to obtain the most trustworthy data possible, researchers use scientific methods in studying factors related to learning and teaching. For a great variety of reasons, few experimenters overcome all the myriad difficulties involved in doing research on education. It may therefore be helpful for you to keep in mind the criteria commonly used in evaluating reports of experimental evidence. A typical article giving the results of a study usually has a brief introductory note explaining the purpose or nature of the problem, a description of the subjects, a detailed statement of the methods and procedures used, an explanation of the treatment of the data, and a summary of results, conclusions, and implications. In the spaces below briefly describe a criterion (or criteria) for roughly evaluating the adequacy of a research report in terms of the following factors:

Subjects

_____

_____

_____

_____

_____

Procedures and methods

_____

_____

_____

_____

Results, conclusions, and implications

_____

_____

_____

_____

_____

_____

Concepts

1. Jerome Bruner concisely describes many of the basic problems of education in his book *The Process of Education* (1960b). One of the most important points he analyzes is transfer. In the following space tell what Bruner means when he says that "general transfer is at the heart of the educational process," and describe some of the problems of teaching so as to encourage general transfer.

Why does Bruner consider transfer to be "at the heart of the educational process"?

_____

_____

_____

_____

_____

What does Bruner suggest must be done in order to teach for transfer?

_____

_____

_____

_____

2. The fact that psychology is a science and teaching is an art can cause trouble for the educator who attempts to combine them. J. M. Stephens has suggested a compromise solution. In the spaces below describe the differences between a *teacher-theorist* and a *teacher-practitioner* (as noted by Stephens), and explain why knowledge of these differences may reduce pressure and confusion as you begin your career as a teacher.

What are key differences between a teacher-theorist and a teacher-practitioner?

_____

_____

_____

_____

How might awareness of these differences reduce pressure on a teacher?

_____

_____

_____

_____

_____

3. In addition to Stephens's observations on the theorist-practitioner theme, a point of view developed by Arthur Coladarci might be taken into account as you try to balance the art and science aspects of teaching. In the space below explain and give an example of how you might put into practice Coladarci's suggestion that you think of teaching as *testing-of-hypothesis behavior.*

Principles

In his *Talks to Teachers,* William James analyzed some of the problems which arise because of the art and science aspects of teaching. He urged teachers to follow their own inclinations but still take into account the well-established findings of scientists. In the space below summarize the general guidelines he offered for expressing your individuality in teaching while at the same time utilizing what scientists have discovered about teaching.

Theories

J. M. Stephens's recently proposed theory of *spontaneous schooling* is an outgrowth of his previous speculations about the teacher as a theorist and a practitioner. (It is also related to the observations of William James regarding science and the art of teaching.) Understanding this theory may help you reconcile conflicts as you attempt to teach in a manner which is consistent with research data in education and psychology. In the following spaces describe the kinds of evidence that led Stephens to develop the theory of spontaneous schooling, and then note why this theory might provide reassurance and peace of mind for you when you begin to teach.

What kinds of evidence led to the development of the theory?

_____

_____

_____

_____

_____

How might awareness of the theory of spontaneous schooling contribute to your peace of mind as a teacher?

_____

_____

_____

_____

Methodology

1. In discussing the methods of science, one may distinguish between *theoretical-deductive* and *empirical-inductive* modes of thought. Lack of awareness of the differences between these two general approaches to scientific study, as well as the fact that not all problems *can* be studied or all applications made in a theoretical-deductive fashion, has caused considerable confusion and misunderstanding. In the following spaces tell how each approach is put into practice, explain why psychologists are more or less forced to use the empirical approach, and note some difficulties often encountered when a teacher tries to find a scientifically substantiated answer to a problem of pedagogy.

How are the theoretical-deductive and empirical-inductive approaches put into practice?

Theoretical-deductive

_____

_____

_____

_____

Empirical-inductive

_____

_____

_____

_____

_____

Why must psychologists use the empirical approach?

_____

_____

_____

What difficulties will you face if you attempt to find a scientifically substantiated answer to a teaching problem?

_____

_____

_____

_____

2. It will be desirable for you to have confidence and enthusiasm when
you set about putting any conception of teaching into practice. However, for
reasons stressed by J. M. Stephens and Arthur Coladarci, it also will be
desirable to try to assess the effectiveness of your efforts in an objective, tenta-
tive manner, because personal involvement in an undertaking often predisposes
the individual to engage in wishful thinking and unsystematic theorizing. In
keeping with the theorist-practitioner theme, explain in the space below how
you might use some of the attitudes and methods of scientists to avoid the pitfalls of personal involvement when you take stock of your teaching techniques.

_____

_____

_____

_____

Suggestions for Further Reading, Thinking, and Discussion

1–1   Examining a Review of Research Studies

Chapter 1 offers a description of the empirical-inductive approach, together with an explanation of why this is the general method of science used by most psychologists. Psychologists are interested in behavior, but not only is every human being different from every other human being; the behavior of the same person varies with each situation and changes over time. Consequently, the psychologist is compelled to observe relatively circumscribed bits of human or animal behavior, take note of the circumstances, and try to build theories from the accumulated evidence. Most theories in psychology, then, are based on a series of related studies; it is extremely rare for a single experiment to "establish" a principle in the behavioral sciences. You will more completely understand the way related studies are combined and compared if you browse through one of the professional journals which specialize in summarizing research on a particular topic. Three of these journals are:

Review of Educational Research, published five times a year by the American Educational Research Association. Each issue summarizes the research on a single topic.

Annual Review of Psychology, which is just that: an annual publication in which a specialist in each of several areas of psychology reviews significant studies that appeared during a given year.

Psychological Bulletin, a journal published six times a year. Most issues of the *Bulletin* contain a detailed summary of research conducted on one or more topics.

For this project, consult one of these journals, note the date and volume number, and give a brief synopsis of a chapter or an article that strikes you as relevant to your own interests, grade level, and subject. You might concentrate on final conclusions and implications (including any implications for your own teaching). In your report use the following outline:

Author(s)

Name of journal

Date and volume

Article or chapter read (give title and pages)

Conclusions of article

Implications noted by the author

Implications (if any) for your own teaching

1–2   Reading an Experimental Study in a Professional Journal in Psychology

As a supplement or alternative to exercise 1–1, find an article in a professional journal in psychology that describes specific experiments. This will permit you to get some direct experience with the raw material of psychology, the building blocks which are eventually combined to establish a principle or theory. You may consult either a journal (such as *Child Development,* the *Journal of Educational Psychology,* the *Journal of Educational Research,* or the *Journal of Experimental Education*) or a book of readings in educational psychology. Several dozen such collections of readings are in print. They consist of articles considered by the editor to be of special importance and relevance to teachers. You will probably find several appropriate volumes in your college library. Browse through one of the journals or one of the books of readings until you see an article describing an experiment which appears relevant to your own interests, grade level, and subject. Then write an abstract of the article following the outline below:

Author(s) of article

Name of article

Journal in which article appears (including date, volume number, and pages)

Purpose (or description of problem)

Subjects

Procedure (or methods)

Treatment of data

Results

Conclusions

Are there any criticisms that you can make of the procedure or of the conclusions?

What inferences for your own teaching can you draw from this experiment (if any)?

Would you be willing to change your methods of teaching on the strength of this one article? Explain your answer.

1–3   Reading a Nonexperimental Article in a Professional Journal

In addition to descriptions of actual experiments, nonexperimental or "discussion" articles are published regularly in a variety of professional journals, including *American Psychologist, Elementary School Journal, Educational Leadership, Harvard Educational Review, School & Society, Teachers College*

Record. If you look through a volume of one of these journals, you will discover the nature of typical discussion articles on psychology and education. Read an article that you feel is relevant to your own interests, grade level, and subject, and then write a synopsis of the arguments of the author(s). If any of these arguments are pertinent to your own theorizing about teaching, briefly analyze your thoughts. Follow the outline below:

Author(s) of article

Name of article

Journal in which article appeared (including date, volume number, and pages)

Synopsis of arguments presented

Your reactions to the arguments

1–4   Reacting to a Section of Bruner's "The Process of Education"

In *The Process of Education* (1960b) (available as a Vintage paperback), Jerome Bruner discusses four major themes: (1) "the role of structure in learning and how it may be made central in teaching," (2) readiness, (3) the nature of intuition, and (4) "the desire to learn and how it may be stimulated." Each theme is discussed in a separate (short) chapter. Read one of these chapters and write a brief résumé of Bruner's arguments. You might discuss such things as: points which impressed you, points you disagree with, ideas that seemed vague or unrealistic or inconsistent, ideas you think you might be able to use in your own teaching. An example of one of the statements you might find provocative is to be found in Chapter 3: "We begin with the hypothesis that any subject can be taught effectively in some intellectually honest form to any child at any stage of development." If this seems hard to accept, read what Bruner has to say—and see if he is able to win you over. In writing your report, follow this outline:

Chapter selected

Résumé of chapter

Reactions

1–5   Sampling the Wit and Wisdom of Jacques Barzun

Chapter 2 of the text mentions some differences between humanists and scientists. Jacques Barzun—a professor of history who later became Provost of Columbia University—is a humanist with a capital H, and he has written at length about what he regards as disadvantages of a scientific approach to education. If you are intrigued by these notions about humanists and scientists, you might sample Barzun's observations. (He has great style and a rapier-like wit.) The first three chapters of *Teacher in America* (1944) include a liberal selection of views on education and many criticisms of those who attempt to make it scientific. Further comments on the relationship between the art of teaching and the impact of education on the development of the intellect are to be found in his later book, *The House of Intellect* (1960). There is a particularly stimulating section on pages 18–30 of the latter, including this assertion: "The intellectual class . . . has been captivated by art, overawed by science and seduced by philanthropy." Chapter IV, "Education Without Instruction," is also provocative, as evidenced by a statement from its opening paragraphs: "There is, there can be, no such thing as a good school."

In his most recent book, *The American University* (subtitled "How It Runs, Where It Is Going"), Barzun analyzes the ills of higher education in America. Here are some comments from Chapter 3, "Students or Victims?":

> The belief that a curriculum can be devised and kept relevant to the present is an illusion: whose present, in the first place, and relevant for how long? Students differ in tastes, knowledge, and emotional orientation. What concerns (or "excites") one four-year generation will bore the next, as anyone can verify by reference to popular music. And so it is with literature, politics, and the current view of creeds and crises.
>
> If a university is not to become an educational weather vane, a sort of weekly journal published orally by aging Ph.D.'s, it must avoid all "relevance" of the obvious sort. The spirit of its teaching will be relevant if its members are good scholars and really teach. Nearly everywhere there is enough free choice among courses so that no student is imprisoned for long in anything he cannot make relevant, if he will only forget the fantasy of instant utility. That fantasy is in fact what rules the world of credentials and qualifications which he so rightly kicks against. (1968, pp. 71–72)

If any of these excerpts interest you, get hold of a copy of one of these books, read the suggested sections (or another of your choice), give a brief résumé of Barzun's arguments, and finish up with your own reactions.

1–6   Tuning in on Some of William James's "Talks to Teachers"

Chapter 1 uses some observations of William James as a framework for contrasting and highlighting the art and science aspects of teaching. These excerpts are taken from *Talks to Teachers,* published in 1899. In his introduction to the paperback reprint of this book (1958), Paul Woodring says, "No writer before or since his time has quite equalled James' gift for making psychology interesting and understandable." This is high praise indeed, and you are likely to enjoy dipping into *Talks to Teachers.* If you obtain the paperback edition, read Woodring's introduction, which gives some enlightening background about James and how his ideas relate to present-day education. You are also urged to read Chapter 1, "Psychology and the Teaching Art." In addition, the Talks to Students at the end of the book are fascinating. There are three of these talks: "The Gospel of Relaxation" (offering "gay nineties" readers advice on how to cope with the breakneck pace of American life), "On a Certain Blindness in Human Beings" (which contains excerpts from the writings of Stevenson, Wordsworth, Whitman, and Tolstoy), and "What Makes Life Significant."

As you read James, note your reactions in a general way—picking and choosing and commenting on ideas which impress you. You will probably gain more from doing this if you make allowance for the fact that James wrote the book more than seventy years ago. It might be interesting to compare the observations of a "free-thinking" educator of 1900 vintage with the opinions of current educators. Keep in mind, too, that many of James's statements on principles of psychology and pedagogy may seem naive or puzzling because psychology was an extremely new science when *Talks to Teachers* was written.

1–7 Learning More about Stephens's Theory of Spontaneous Schooling

J. M. Stephens has devoted his long professional life to the study of educational psychology. His concern with the science *and* art aspects of teaching was first expressed when he discussed the distinctions between the teacher-theorist and the teacher-practitioner in *Educational Psychology* (1951). Sixteen years later the same concern was put differently when he proposed his theory of spontaneous schooling, described in *The Process of Schooling* (1967). This relatively short paperback is both interesting and thought-provoking. If you are unable to read the entire book, you might peruse Chapter 1, "The Argument in Brief"; Chapter 3, "The Origins and Social Role of the School"; Chapter 6, "Spontaneous Tendencies and Scholastic Achievement"; Chapter 8, "The Effective Teacher: His Characteristics and Place in Society"; or Chapter 11, "Prescription for Relaxation." In case you sample any of these chapters, summarize Stephens's observations and then add your own reactions.

1–8 Testing a Hypothesis

To get into the habit of functioning as a teacher-theorist, you might make an effort to follow the suggestion of Arthur Coladarci and think of teaching as testing-of-hypothesis behavior. If you have the opportunity to act as a teacher aide or the equivalent during the time you are taking the course for which this

Study Guide was designed, pick out an idea, set up a hypothesis, and test it.

For example, a teacher aide in a first grade was impressed by the concept of individual differences. She got to thinking about the standard wide-lined paper traditionally used in teaching lettering in the primary grades. Hypothesizing that not all children would be inclined to print letters of exactly the same size, she obtained paper with lines of varying widths and permitted the students to take their choice. Some children preferred relatively narrow lines as opposed to the standard wide lines. She then tried to determine whether the use of narrow lines actually improved printing skill. Although unable to do a completely scientific job, she got enough feedback to convince her that some children benefit from the opportunity to print on a smaller scale than others.

Another example: Think of a new unit or approach to teaching as a hypothesis by saying to yourself, "If I ask them to respond to this material in class discussion, I ought to get a better response than I did when I used a lecture approach." This sort of thinking will permit you to make the most of Coladarci's suggestion that "ideas and decisions about method and curriculum are to be held hypothetically, continuously tested and continuously revised if necessary."

You should be aware of the limitations of functioning as a teacher-theorist, however. J. M. Stephens has pointed out that the scientist tries to avoid pitfalls in establishing relationships by using sufficient unselected cases, by using a control group, by being precise in observing, and by exploring all possible hypotheses. You may not be able to meet the first of these conditions in setting up an experimental approach to teaching since you will have no choice about the pupils in your classes. It may also be impossible to have a control group. Furthermore, you may find it impractical to apply the results of a teaching experiment with one group to a future group because no two classes are alike. (As a matter of fact, the same class may not react the same way the second time around.) Nevertheless, you can attempt to be precise and objective in observing, and keep in mind the importance of considering alternative explanations to be tested by further experimentation.

Write down a hypothesis about teaching and outline how you might test it in at least a somewhat scientific manner. If you can, test it out on a class of public school pupils. If this is not possible, you might try to function vicariously as a teacher by identifying with one of your college instructors as he presents a lecture or guides a discussion. In the event the presentation goes over well, think about it and analyze why it worked. If one approach doesn't work as well as another, dream up some alternate hypotheses you might test if *you* were the teacher.

Whether your hypothesis testing was real or imaginary, describe how you did it, and comment on your results.

STUDY GUIDE

Background for
a Teacher-Theorist

Key Points

Trends

Philosophical conflicts among educators, humanists, and scientists due to evolution from normal schools to teachers colleges to liberal arts colleges

"Cult of efficiency" in education due to impact of business (Callahan)

Experiments

Conditioning of dog to salivate when bell rings (Pavlov)

Shaping of behavior of rat and pigeon by reinforcement (Skinner)

Solving of stick problem by ape through insight (Köhler)

Concepts

Zeitgeist

Contingencies of reinforcement

Gestalt

Readiness

Cognitive dissonance, Hawthorne effect, experimenter bias effect

Theories

Behaviorism (Watson)

Skinner's version of S-R associationism culminating in programmed instruction

Bruner's form of cognitive field theory leading to his type of discovery approach

"Natural" and guided-experience views of development

The environmentalist's and the hereditarian's views of determinism

Perceptual view of behavior (Combs and Snygg)

Chapter Contents

Testing and Organizing Your Knowledge of Key Points in Chapter 2

Trends

1. The way different professors teach courses in their specialties reflects the fact that there are many approaches to higher education. Why professors of literature, biology, or education (for example) teach as they do will become more understandable if you take into account the history of teacher education in the United States. In the following spaces describe the evolution of teacher training institutions from normal schools into colleges, and within this frame of reference note the somewhat conflicting philosophies espoused by educators, humanists, and scientists. (One way to do this would be to imagine how a professor from each of these areas might argue if he were asked to serve on a committee that was charged with developing a new curriculum for credential candidates.)

Description of evolution of normal school into college

_____

_____

_____

_____

_____

Education professor's view of education

_____

_____

_____

_____

Humanist's view of education

_____

_____

_____

_____

Scientist's view of education

_____

_____

_____

_____

Think about courses you have taken in the humanities, the sciences, and education. Can you pick out a professor within each category who seemed to endorse the arguments you just summarized? Do you favor one particular emphasis over the others? If so, are you "faithful" to the position described for your general area of interest—e.g., if you have majored in and/or will be teaching a science, are you partial to that point of view? If not, analyze *why* you are "unfaithful."

2. Trends in education reflect trends in a culture, and some observers feel that many aspects of American education reflect our national preoccupation with technological efficiency. This is the opinion of Raymond Callahan in *Education and the Cult of Efficiency* (1962). In the following space analyze Callahan's suggestion that a "cult of efficiency" in American education has

evolved out of respect and admiration for business methods in a technological society, and comment on how awareness of this possibility may assist you to understand certain aspects of contemporary education in the United States.

_____

_____

_____

_____

_____

Key Experiments

1. You should be able to explain the nature of the experiment which more or less started the development of the theory of teaching endorsed by the majority of American psychologists. In the space below give a capsule description of Pavlov's experiment and tell how it served as the basis for learning theories which stress *associations* between stimuli and responses.

_____

_____

_____

_____

_____

2. You should also be able to explain the classic experiment which is the key to Gestalt psychology and thus to a theory of learning endorsed by a sizable minority of American psychologists. In the space below describe how the experiment involving an ape, two sticks, and a banana established a principle which is the cornerstone of cognitive-field theory.

_____

_____

_____

_____

Concepts

1. In *A History of Experimental Psychology* (1950), Edwin G. Boring emphasizes the importance of taking into account the culture of the times in speculating about the development of a theory. Theories of education are no exception. In the spaces below comment on how the *Zeitgeist* of America in the 1950's might have influenced the theories of B. F. Skinner. You might also try to relate the Zeitgeist of this country in the 1970's to current controversies and trends in education.

How the Zeitgeist of the 1950's might have influenced B. F. Skinner

_____

_____

_____

_____

_____

How the Zeitgeist of the 1970's may be affecting current trends in education

_____

_____

_____

_____

_____

2. S-R associationists use the term *contingencies of reinforcement* to explain a key aspect of their theory of learning. In the space below explain what is meant by this term.

_____

_____

_____

3. Cognitive-field theorists use the term *Gestalt* to explain a key aspect of their learning theory. In the space below explain what is meant by this term.

_____

_____

_____

_____

4. Basic to an evaluation of views on development is the concept of *readiness*. In the space below explain what is meant by this term.

_____

_____

_____

_____

_____

5. When you theorize about almost any aspect of teaching, you will need to consider the possible impact of three psychological mechanisms which will complicate your speculations: *cognitive dissonance,* the *Hawthorne effect,* and the *experimenter bias effect.* In the spaces below define and give an example of each of these mechanisms. After each definition and example indicate how awareness of the mechanisms might help you overcome tendencies to misinterpret your own observations or experimental evidence provided by others.

Definition, example, and comments on cognitive dissonance

_____

_____

_____

_____

_____

_____

_____

Definition, example, and comments on the Hawthorne effect

_____

_____

_____

_____

_____

_____

Definition, example, and comments on the experimenter bias effect

_____

_____

_____

_____

_____

_____

Theories

1. One of the earliest schools of psychology to develop in the United States was *behaviorism*. Understanding why John B. Watson, its founder, chose that word to describe his theory of psychology will assist you to comprehend the tenets of S-R associationism since associationism is an outgrowth of behaviorism. While contemporary behaviorist-associationists do not adhere as rigidly to Watson's premise as he did himself, they endorse the same general idea. In the spaces below explain why Watson picked the word *behaviorism,* and then tell how a contemporary behaviorist-associationist might set up experiments in accordance with Watson's original guidelines.

Why Watson chose the term *behaviorism*

_____

_____

_____

_____

How a contemporary behaviorist-associationist might set up an experiment

_____

_____

_____

_____

_____

_____

_____

2. The two basic techniques of teaching which are emphasized throughout the text are B. F. Skinner's method of *programmed instruction* and Jerome Bruner's version of the *discovery approach*. To understand the reasoning behind them, you should be able to explain how each man was influenced by learning theory. In the spaces below describe how Skinner's allegiance to S-R associationism affected his development of programmed learning and how Bruner's attraction to cognitive-field theory caused him to favor the discovery approach. (In each case describe an experiment which served as a basis for the technique developed and tell how it relates to the method of instruction.)

How Skinner's allegiance to associationism led to programmed instruction

_____

_____

_____

_____

_____

How Bruner's leaning toward field theory led to his preference for the discovery approach

_____

_____

_____

_____

3. In speculating about individual personality and behavior, theorists take into account the relative influence of heredity and environment. In the text the views of B. F. Skinner and Aldous Huxley illustrate the kinds of arguments endorsed by those who believe that one force exerts more influence than the other. Many of the differences of opinion between Skinner and Huxley focus on the single question: Is man a free agent? This question may have considerable significance for you as a teacher since how you feel about it may influence your entire philosophy of education. If it seems to you that man is primarily the product of contingencies of reinforcement, you will try to arrange experiences so as to shape behavior in a desired direction. If you believe, on the other hand, that an individual inherits predispositions which may eventually be expressed in unique ways, you may wish to allow as much freedom as possible for each child to develop in his own fashion. To clarify your

thinking on this question, summarize the major arguments of Skinner and Huxley on the question of determinism and man as a free agent.

Skinner's main arguments in support of an environmental interpretation of determinism

_____

_____

_____

_____

_____

Huxley's arguments in favor of a genetic interpretation of determinism

_____

_____

_____

_____

_____

To deepen your thoughts on these arguments, ask yourself how the literary style of Mark Twain might be explained by Skinner and Huxley. What key factor made Mark Twain the man he was—the environment of life in the Clemens family in Hannibal, Missouri, or a particular and unique set of genes? Some of the problems of attempting to find an either-or answer will emerge when you imagine how Mark Twain might have developed if he had been born in New York City. Then ask yourself why other boys (particularly Orion Clemens, Samuel's brother) who grew up in Hannibal did not achieve the literary fame Twain did. If you like, record your thoughts in the space below.

_____

_____

_____

_____

4. Related to speculations about determinism are views regarding development. At the present time some theorists favor exposing children to scientifically planned sequences of experiences in an effort to speed up and shape development. Other theorists stress the idea of "natural" readiness. In the

spaces below describe the concepts endorsed by the *guided-experience* advocates and by those who prefer a *"natural" development* philosophy. After each description, give an example of a technique of pedagogy which could be used with that point of view.

Concepts and techniques of the guided-experience view of development

_____

_____

_____

_____

_____

_____

_____

Concepts and techniques of the "natural" view of development

_____

_____

_____

_____

_____

_____

_____

5. Arthur Combs and Donald Snygg join Jerome Bruner in endorsing a cognitive-field theory approach to learning. They explain their preference for a Gestalt approach by proposing a *perceptual* view of behavior, and emphasize some basic distinctions between field theory and associationism. In the spaces below give a brief description of the principles of the perceptual point of view and contrast them with those of behaviorism.

Basic principles of the perceptual point of view

_____

_____

_____

_____

_____

How they differ from the principles emphasized by behaviorists

_____

_____

_____

_____

_____

_____

Suggestions for Further Reading, Thinking, and Discussion

2–1   Assessing the Impact of the History of Teacher Education in America

The courses you must take in order to earn a credential, and the attitudes and beliefs the teachers of these courses have toward education, are in part due to the way teacher education evolved in America. For information about early developments which influenced current practice, read Chapter 6, "The Teachers College in America," in *Let's Talk Sense About Our Schools* (1953) by Paul Woodring, or Chapter 5, "The Education of Teachers," in *A Fourth of a Nation* (1957) by the same author. (The first four chapters of the latter volume supply insight into the conflict between those who espoused "classic" education and those who advocated the "whole child" approach, and show how the debate led to present-day practices in schools.)

If you read any sections of these books, give a brief description of the points made by Woodring, and add any observations of your own. You might include comments on courses or teachers you have had which either uphold or contradict Woodring's views.

2–2   Are Scientists More Effective Than Philosophers?

Scientists emphasize the cumulative nature of scientific knowledge. B. F. Skinner, for example, has pointed out, "Our contemporary writers, artists and philosophers are not appreciably more effective than those of the Golden Age of Greece, yet the average high school student of today understands much more of nature than the greatest of Greek scientists." Skinner attributes this increased effectiveness to the fact that science "is a unique intellectual process which yields remarkable results."

Do you think contemporary writers, artists, and philosophers are more— or less—effective than Shakespeare, Michelangelo, and Aristotle? What explanations can you give for greater or lesser effectiveness—if you think it exists?

The superiority of contemporary scientists over those of even one hundred years ago seems obvious in terms of their accomplishments. But does this mean scientists should take the primary responsibility for determining how scientific knowledge is to be used? If you are intrigued with this question, put your thoughts down in writing.

2–3 Analyzing the Behavioristic View of Determinism

In *Science and Human Behavior* (1953), B. F. Skinner describes the scientist's view of determinism: "We must expect to discover that what a man does is the result of specifiable conditions and that once these conditions have been discovered, we can anticipate and to some extent determine his actions." This statement reflects the idea that in order to improve human behavior, we must be able to predict and control it. Thus, Skinner argues, observations must be restricted to *overt* behavior which can be analyzed with scientific rigor. It is assumed, then, that man is not free—in the sense that he controls his own behavior through nonobservable inner forces. We should concentrate on causes outside of the individual, since only such causes can be manipulated to bring about improvements in behavior. If you find this point of view interesting, read Chapters 1 and 2 and the last chapter of *Science and Human Behavior,* and record your reactions to Skinner's arguments.

2–4 Analyzing the Perceptual Psychologist's View of Behavior

Not all psychologists feel it necessary to restrict observations to *overt* behavior in order to be acceptably scientific. Arthur Combs and Donald Snygg assert, for example, that "the facts of human behavior . . . are not the facts that exist for others, but the facts that exist for the behaver. . . . The data with which we must deal in understanding and changing human relationships, then, are feelings, attitudes, beliefs, and values." In case you want to discover more about the perceptual—as opposed to behavioristic—view of psychology, browse through Chapters 14 and 15 of *Individual Behavior* (1959) by Combs and Snygg and then record your reactions.

2–5 Examining a Humanist's View of Determinism

Aldous Huxley was an eloquent champion of individuality and freedom and a critic of any sort of control over human behavior. He first expressed his views on the dangers of control in his novel *Brave New World* (1932). Twenty-six years later came a collection of essays entitled *Brave New World Revisited* (1958), and still later in the novel *Island* (1962) his conception of a Utopia in which the freedom of the individual would be preserved. If you have ever speculated about the possible dangers of too much control over behavior, you might enjoy reading one of these books. If you do, give a résumé of your reactions.

2–6   Evaluating a Utopia Based on the Principles of Science

In *Walden Two* (1948), B. F. Skinner describes a fictional Utopia based on the principles of his approach to a science of human behavior. It is a fascinating story, and you might read it to see whether you think you would like to live in the sort of world he imagines. What aspects of *Walden Two* strike you as most appealing? What aspects would you find difficult to accept? Do you think real people would react to the Utopia the way the characters in the novel react? Can you come up with an improved Utopia of your own? Record your reactions to any or all of these questions.

2–7   Assessing the Impact of "Efficiency" on American Education

Many schools in this country emphasize efficiency and economy. This emphasis sometimes leads to educational practices which are improvements from one point of view, but undesirable by-products may make life difficult for teachers. The impact of citizens' demands for efficiency and economy in education is discussed in *Education and the Cult of Efficiency* (1962) by Raymond E. Callahan. In the last chapter Callahan sums up his views on the current situation and remarks on factors which tend to cause difficulties and misunderstandings. If you read any sections of this book, give a general analysis of your reactions, or offer your own comments on the pros and cons of making education "efficient."

2–8   Are Teachers "Organization Men"?

In *The Organization Man* (1956), William H. Whyte, Jr., describes the effect of American business methods on our way of life. Part I, "The Ideology of Organization Man," gives a general overview of his analysis. Chapters 7 and 8 concentrate on the impact of business on education, and Part 5, "The Organization Scientist," tells how an organization approach to science and technology tends to limit creativity. The last chapter sums up the case against the organization. If you have ever brooded about the influence of the establishment on the American way of life—and education—you will find sections of *The Organization Man* highly provocative. Record your reactions in the form of general notes or a brief essay.

2–9 Trying to Understand Student Unrest

The most obvious thing about contemporary higher education in America is that many people are dissatisfied with it. You may want to read one or more interpretations of student unrest and/or record your own reactions. *Education and the Barricades* (1968) is a short book by Charles Frankel analyzing the complaints and tactics of student rebels. *The Higher Learning in America: A Reassessment* (1968) by Paul Woodring is a wider treatment of the same topic. While Frankel offers brief suggestions for improvement, Woodring describes a comprehensive educational program designed to correct for what he perceives to be the weaknesses of the present system. Read either of these books, or others on the same subject, and comment on the analysis and recommendations of the authors. Or, if you prefer, write your own diagnosis of the ills of higher education and list your own prescriptions for improvement.

2–10 Reading an Autobiographical Sketch by a Famous Psychologist

Edwin G. Boring has variously expressed his interest in the impact of the Zeitgeist of the times on a theorist. In addition to his book *A History of Experimental Psychology* (1950), he established and/or edited a series of volumes (five so far) consisting of brief autobiographical sketches of famous psychologists. For a description of his own life by one or more of the psychologists mentioned in the text, search for the appropriate volume of *A History of Psychology in Autobiography*. Here is a list of the men already mentioned in the text with the volume of the series in which each one's autobiography appears. (Note: Volumes II and III were edited by Carl Murchison; Volumes IV and V by Boring and others.)

Edward L. Thorndike, Volume III (1936)

John B. Watson, Volume III (1936)

Edwin G. Boring, Volume IV (1952)

B. F. Skinner, Volume V (1967)

(At appropriate places later in this Study Guide your attention will be called to the autobiographies of other psychologists not yet noted in the text.)

Since B. F. Skinner is mentioned more frequently in the text than any other man, his autobiography may be of special interest. This is how it begins:

> My Grandmother Skinner was an uneducated farmer's daughter who put on airs. She was naturally attracted to a young Englishman who came to America in the early 1870's looking for work, and she married him. (He had not found just the work he wanted when he died at the age of ninety.) (Vol. V, p. 387)

If you read any of the sketches, try to relate the background and experiences described to what you know of the man's theories or specialty within psychology. Is the impact of the Zeitgeist apparent?

2–11   Sampling an Article or Feature in a Teachers' Journal

Unless you teach psychology in a high school or junior college, you are hardly likely to refer to professional journals in psychology when your last course in that subject is over. If you do consult professional journals after embarking on your teaching career, they will probably be those written especially for public school teachers of a particular breed. There are dozens of such periodicals, some devoted to all aspects of teaching, some published for specialists in different grade levels and/or subject areas. The following journals are found in an education and psychology section of a typical college library. Glancing through this list, you will probably discover one or more which will be relevant to your own interests.

American Biology Teacher	*Journal of Business Education*
Arithmetic Teacher	*Journal of Health and Physical Education*
Art Educator	*Journal of Reading*
Athletic Journal	*Journal of Research in Music Education*
Childhood Education	*Journal of School Health*
Coach and Athlete	*Journal of Secondary Education*
Education	*Mathematics Teacher*
Education Digest	*Modern Language Journal*
Educational Theatre Journal	*Music in Education*
Elementary English	*Music Journal*
Elementary School Journal	*NEA Journal* (Since 1968, *Today's*
English Journal	*Education*)
English Language Teaching	*Reading Teacher*
Forecast for Home Economists	*Safety Education*
French Review	*Scholastic Coach*
German Quarterly	*School Arts*
Grade Teacher	*School Musician Director and Teacher*
High School Journal	*School Science and Mathematics*
Hispania	*School Shop*
Industrial Arts and Vocational	*Science Educator*
Education	*Science Teacher*
Industrial Arts Teacher	*Social Studies*
The Instructor	*Speech Teacher*

In order to get the flavor of the articles, browse through some recent issues of two or three journals that appear pertinent to your grade level and subject matter. Read one article in its entirety, summarize it, and comment on how you might use the ideas discussed. In judging articles, take into account the hazards of converting theory to practice which are mentioned in the text. For example, consider these questions: (1) Did the author's suggestions seem to be based on data obtained under well-controlled conditions? (2) Did the author back up his views by referring to studies you could read on your own— so that it would be possible to refer to the original data and draw your own conclusions? (3) Was the author relatively objective and impartial in discussing ideas, or did you detect signs of "evangelism" in the sense that he seemed almost totally committed to a particular approach and highly critical of different approaches? (4) Do you think the suggestions offered would work equally well for all teachers and pupils in all situations? If not, why not?

Failing to find an article of interest, you might sample other features of the less formal journals (e.g., *The Instructor, NEA Journal*). For example, read some of the letters to the editor, a book review or two, short pieces presenting specific techniques of teaching that worked especially well for a particular teacher. If you find any of these stimulating, record your impressions and make an estimate as to how valuable a given journal might be to you once you begin to teach. Note: In 1968 the *NEA Journal* became *Today's Education.*

2–12 Developing Wariness of Newspaper and Magazine Reports

Your most fruitful source of new ideas in education and teaching will probably be teachers' journals and teachers' conferences. However, articles about new techniques also appear in newspapers and mass-circulation magazines. While they may serve to alert you to the latest developments, it is usually prudent to reserve judgment until professional sources evaluate them. Most newspaper and magazine reporters are primarily interested in attracting and holding the attention of the reader. They may therefore feel impelled to exaggerate or oversimplify and to rhapsodize about innovations as if they were the panacea for all problems in education. (The same is true of most copywriters for book ads.) An example is the press reaction to Rosenthal and Jacobson's *Pygmalion in the Classroom* (1968), mentioned in Chapter 3. Many reporters implied that the only thing teachers had to do was act as if they *expected* all their students to be above average, and presto! all their students *would* become above average. This was hailed as a breakthrough of tremendous significance. The reporters did not take the trouble (or have the training) to check on the experimental design of the study or analyze the conclusions. Neither did they suggest that until the study had been replicated by others, caution was in order.

Another example is the nonprofessional reviews and book advertisements for *Education and Ecstasy* by George Leonard, ballyhooed as *the* answer to all the ills of education. Some teachers and prospective teachers who were stimulated to buy and read the book were dismayed to discover that although Leonard has a great deal of enthusiasm, he speculates most about what education *might* be like in the year 2000—and under ideal circumstances at that.

To check on often misleading publicity, be on the alert for newspaper and magazine articles which hail the latest revolutionary cure-all for education, or for advertisements of new books on education. Then compare them to evaluations of the same techniques or publications presented in teachers' journals. Or, in the absence of such reports, do a critical analysis yourself. How much faith are you prepared to put in a reporter's interpretation of an innovation in education which is described in a newspaper or magazine? Do you detect unsubstantiated claims or shaky generalizations? Does the reporter get carried away with enthusiasm? Does he give the impression of knowing what really goes in a typical public school classroom? Are you willing to invest $5 to $10 in a new book on the strength of advertisements?

2–13   Becoming Aware That There Are Almost Always Two Sides to Arguments in Education and Psychology

Because of the impact of personal involvement and the nature of cognitive dissonance, the Hawthorne effect, and the experimenter bias effect, a new development in education is often presented as the best way to solve a particular problem of teaching, and criticisms or alternate techniques are ignored or minimized. A man who has devoted several years to perfecting a novel technique naturally begins to think of it as a "cause," and to defend it against criticism and reject counterproposals made by others. This tendency to favor a certain point of view often leads to a polarization of arguments. Several general dichotomies are discussed in Chapter 2: associationism–field theory, heredity–environment, "natural" development–guided experience. Throughout the text, an effort has been made to give both sides of key issues so that you can make up your own mind. (It must be noted, however, that the author is not immune to the human frailties which lead to personal affinities for certain ideas in education, and that some points of view are favored over others in the way the discussion in the text is presented.)

As you read about new developments in education, remain aware of the polarizing or dichotomizing tendencies which stem from the psychological mechanisms mentioned above. If a theorist argues in favor of one approach, keep an eye out for counterarguments. (In the text and in this Study Guide, you are referred to many articles or books setting forth a point of view different from that emphasized.) The *NEA Journal* (*Today's Education*) often presents one or more educators arguing for a position and also one or more arguing against it. And quite often critical observations from the "other side" in the form either of letters to the editor or of articles giving follow-up critiques follow an original article. To get experience with this aspect of theorizing about education and psychology, read one of the differences-of-opinion articles in the *NEA Journal,* or browse through a bound set of some other teachers' journal for a given year looking for letters or articles which summarize counterarguments to ideas presented earlier. When making such a comparison, list the arguments for and against and then record your own position on the subject being debated.

2–14 Examining a Concise Description of Philosophical Assumptions and Schools of Psychology

Gordon W. Allport was one of the first psychologists to call attention to differences between associationism and field theory, particularly their opposing basic assumptions regarding the relationship between philosophy and science. In *Becoming* (1955), Allport provides a concise analysis of problems of studying personality. In the first twenty pages of this short book he succinctly describes the concerns of humanists, traces S-R associationism to the views of John Locke (including the tabula rasa concept), explains the derivation of Gestalt principles from the observations of Gottfried Leibnitz, and comments on what he considers to be the primary goal of psychology. In a section which begins on page 83 he discusses freedom and determinism, and in the Epilogue he makes some observations about reconciling aspects of an associationist approach with the principles of democracy. If you are not completely clear about some of the basic differences between associationism and field theory and/or would like to speculate about some of the philosophical assumptions involved in different conceptions of science, you are urged to read these sections in *Becoming* and note your reactions.

Part Two / Development

STUDY GUIDE

Development: Principles and Theories

Key Points

Sequences and Trends	Egocentric speech, socialized speech (Piaget)
	Moral realism, moral relativism (Piaget)
	Intellectual development: sensorimotor, preoperational, concrete operations, formal operations (Piaget)
	Enactive, iconic, and symbolic thought (Bruner)
	Revival of techniques developed by Montessori

Experiments and Studies	Walking by cradleboard babies at same age as others (Dennis and Dennis)
	Faster skill learning by older preschoolers (Hilgard)
	Imprinting of any moving object by newborn goslings (Lorenz)
	50 percent of intelligence by age 4—speculative hypothesis (Bloom)
	Higher scores by pupils labeled bright—suspect data (Rosenthal and Jacobson)

Concepts	Standardization groups and their limitations	Group, or actuarial, prediction
	Overlap	Critical periods
	Prehension	Operation (Piaget)

Principles	Development as a product of maturation and learning
	Less predictable behavior in older children
	Progression from general to specific responses
	Irregular nature of short-term growth
	Variance in rates of development
	Organization, adaptation, assimilation, accommodation (Piaget)

Theories	Developmental tasks (Havighurst)	
	Oral, anal, and genital stages; fixation by traumatic experience (Freud)	
	Children's resiliency, and development by repeated experiences (Anderson)	
	Development (Gesell)	Intellectual development (Piaget)

40

Chapter Contents

The Age-Level Approach and Its Limitations

Weaknesses of the Standardization Group
Group Prediction, Not Individual Prediction

General Principles of Development

Development as a Product of Maturation and Learning
Less Predictable Pattern of Development with Increasing Age
Progression from General to Specific Responses
Continuous Long-Term Development but Irregular Short-Term Growth
Variance in Rates of Development

Two Current Views of Readiness

Origin of Concept of "Natural" Readiness and of Concept of Critical Periods
Critical Period Theory: Enriched Early Experience Boosts I.Q.

Theories of Gesell

His Background and Criticisms of His Work
The Gesell Institute Readiness Tests

The Impact of Expectation

Theories of Piaget

His Background and Early Theories
Most Comprehensive Theory: Stages of Intellectual Development

Bruner's Theory of Instruction

Recap of the Development Debate

Testing and Organizing Your Knowledge of Key Points in Chapter 3

Sequences and Trends

1. Jean Piaget has devoted his professional life to studying sequences in children's development of language and thought. One of his earliest descriptions implied that there is a developmental change from *egocentric* to *socialized* speech. Even though subsequent research has indicated that children do not manifest the rather sudden and qualitative switch from one to the other at about the age of seven or eight that Piaget suggested, the distinction between the two types of speech does appear to exist, and it does have significance for teachers. (The pedagogical meaning of the distinction is noted in Chapter 4.) In the spaces below describe what Piaget means by egocentric and socialized speech.

Basic characteristics of egocentric speech

_____

_____

_____

_____

Basic characteristics of socialized speech

_____

_____

_____

_____

2. Another of Piaget's descriptions of developmental changes emphasized a changeover from *moral realism* to *moral relativism*. As with egocentric and socialized speech, it seemed to Piaget that a somewhat abrupt switch from one to the other took place. (The more mature understanding of morality came toward the end of the elementary school years.) Controlled observations indicated that there *are* recognizable differences between moral realists and relativists, but also that the transition from one status to the other is gradual rather than abrupt. (The significance of the differences will be discussed in Chapter 4.) In the spaces below state the basic differences between a moral realist and a moral relativist.

Moral realist

_____

_____

_____

_____

Moral relativist

_____

_____

_____

_____

3. Piaget's most comprehensive theory describes an elaborate sequence of stages in intellectual development. These four stages constitute one of the most important and frequently discussed sets of ideas in contemporary education, and every well-informed teacher should be familiar with them. In the space below state the term Piaget uses for each stage, the approximate age at which a typical child reaches each stage, and the kind of thought characteristic of each stage.

Stage of Development	*Age Range*	*Kind of Thinking*
a.		
b.		
c.		
d.		

4. Jerome Bruner's description of the stages of intellectual development is very similar to but less elaborate than Piaget's. Since the views of Bruner are mentioned in several chapters in the text, you should be able to give a brief outline of his developmental stages in cognition. Awareness of the meaning of the words he uses may help you not only learn Bruner's classification but also gain insight into the stages described by Piaget. In the space below give Bruner's words for the three stages in his conception of intellectual development and explain their significance. (What do they mean? Why did Bruner

select them?) You should also know the approximate age at which a child reaches each stage.

Name of Stage   *Explanation for Name*   *Approximate Age Range*

a. _____

_____

_____

_____

b. _____

_____

_____

_____

c. _____

_____

_____

_____

5. As with fashion, trends in education often go in cycles. Ideas favored at one time are dropped only to reemerge later. Sixty years ago, Maria Montessori touched off a revolution in preschool education. Thirty years ago "natural" development became the object of attention and preschool education was deemphasized to some extent. In the 1960's, the pendulum swung back toward nursery schools again, and the theories of Montessori are more popular now than they were even during her lifetime. Awareness of why Montessori schools have become almost a fad may help you understand current trends and controversies in education. In the space below explain why Montessori has suddenly achieved new fame sixty years after the publication of her first book on preschool education.

_____

_____

_____

_____

_____

_____

Experiments and Studies

1. In the 1930's, several studies were directed to determining the relative effectiveness of early and late training. An experiment by Josephine Hilgard to discover the impact of training given to three-year-old children early and late in the school year is considered a classic. Since there is a great deal of discussion at present on the desirability of formally instructing children as early as the first few months of life, the Hilgard study (and others like it) provides important background information. In the spaces below describe the experimental design, conclusions, and implications of the Hilgard study.

Experimental design and conclusions of the Hilgard study

_____

_____

_____

_____

_____

Implications of the Hilgard study

_____

_____

_____

_____

_____

2. One reason for the interest in early training is the evidence that there are *critical periods* in the development of many organisms. The original study which led to this concept was conducted by the Austrian naturalist Konrad Lorenz, who observed *imprinting* in goslings. In the spaces below describe imprinting and explain how it relates to interest in critical periods. Then tell what is meant by critical periods and indicate how acceptance of their existence might influence one's planning of educational experiences.

Explanation of imprinting

_____

_____

_____

_____

How imprinting relates to interest in critical periods

_____

_____

_____

_____

_____

Explanation of critical period concept and how its endorsement might influence educational planning

_____

_____

_____

_____

_____

_____

3. Benjamin Bloom became interested in the work of Lorenz and in related observations made by René Spitz, who described *marasmus,* and Martin Deutsch, who established preschools for disadvantaged children. Such studies and others like them prompted Bloom to conduct an analysis of research data bearing on critical periods in human development, particularly intellectual development. He reported his findings in *Stability and Change in Human Characteristics,* emphasizing the rapid rate of early intellectual growth and the importance of a stimulating preschool environment. Since Bloom's book has become the basis for many current educational innovations and theories (including aspects of Head Start programs), a well-informed teacher should be aware of its major theme. In the spaces below summarize Bloom's conclusions regarding intellectual development and comment on their significance and implications.

Summary of Bloom's conclusions

_____

_____

_____

_____

_____

Significance and implications of these conclusions

_____
_____
_____
_____
_____
_____
_____
_____

4. When *Stability and Change in Human Characteristics* was first published, Bloom's conclusions were wholeheartedly endorsed by many psychologists and educators. Since that time evidence from various sources indicates that Bloom overgeneralized to some extent. If you wanted to argue against complete acceptance of Bloom's views on the crucial importance of the first few years of life, what evidence could you cite to back up your arguments? Summarize it in the space below.

_____
_____
_____
_____
_____
_____
_____
_____
_____

5. In *Pygmalion in the Classroom,* Rosenthal and Jacobson describe one of the most controversial experiments of recent years. This report attributes great significance to the Pygmalion effect (or self-fulfilling prophecy), a concept of potential importance to all teachers. In the spaces below describe the experimental design and conclusions of the Rosenthal and Jacobson study, explain how this led to emphasis on the self-fulfilling prophecy, and summarize some of the criticisms which have been made of the study.

Experimental design and conclusions of the Rosenthal and Jacobson study

_____

_____

_____

_____

_____

_____

_____

_____

Significance of the self-fulfilling prophecy

_____

_____

_____

_____

_____

_____

_____

_____

Summary of criticisms of the Rosenthal and Jacobson study

_____

_____

_____

_____

_____

_____

_____

_____

Concepts

1. In establishing age-level trends, since psychologists cannot observe *all* children, they base their descriptions on a few selected children. As you interpret age-level characteristics of any sort you should remain aware of this

fact. In the space below indicate the nature of *standardization groups* and tell how the sample of children observed may limit the applicability of age-level descriptions.

_____

_____

_____

_____

_____

_____

_____

2. The final three stages in Piaget's concept of intellectual development emphasize *operations*. If you are to understand the significance of these stages, and why Piaget designated them as he did, you should be able to explain what an operation is. In the space below define what Piaget means when he speaks of operations.

_____

_____

_____

_____

_____

3. The behavioral scientist aims to predict behavior so that he may in turn control behavior. It is sometimes difficult to use age-level characteristics to predict and control the behavior of individual pupils, however, because of the nature of *group* (or actuarial) *prediction*. In the space below explain why a teacher might need to use age-level descriptions in making *general* plans to anticipate or control the behavior of some or most pupils, as opposed to predicting the behavior of individual pupils.

_____

_____

_____

_____

_____

4. When age-level characteristics which can be measured with some precision are depicted graphically, the diagram clearly demonstrates the concept of *overlap* among children of different age levels. In the spaces below draw a diagram showing overlap and then explain the significance of the diagram as far as interpretations of age-level characteristics are concerned. (In the diagram you might superimpose a hypothetical distribution of the weights of 500 twelve-year-old boys over a hypothetical distribution of the weights of 500 thirteen-year-old boys.)

Diagram depicting an example of overlap

Explanation of the significance of the diagram

Principles

1. The pattern of development becomes less predictable with increasing age. A study by Dennis and Dennis which compared the age of walking of Indian babies who were reared in two different tribes—one using the traditional cradleboard and one not—was mentioned in the text as leading to the establishment of this principle. In the space below explain (on the basis of the Dennis and Dennis study) why the behavior of a one-year-old is likely to be much more predictable than that of a fifteen-year-old.

2. Development often proceeds from general to specific responses. Analyses of *prehension* illustrate this principle of maturation. In the spaces below describe how prehension evolves and then comment on the wider applications of the principle of development illustrated by prehension.

Description of development of prehension

_____

_____

_____

_____

_____

Wider implications of principle illustrated by prehension

_____

_____

_____

_____

_____

3. General trends in the overall development of a child often emerge in a clear-cut way. However, during a typical nine-month period (such as a school year), development may appear to be irregular and unpredictable. As a teacher you will be aware that certain kinds of development in certain children are "irregular" to a baffling extent. In the space below explain one type of exception to the overall forward thrust of growth which you may need to take into account. (Suppose, for example, that a first-grade boy who had overcome a tendency to suck his thumb early in the year backslides shortly after the arrival of a baby sister. What general type of irregularity in development does this illustrate?)

_____

_____

_____

_____

_____

Theories

1. Robert Havighurst has suggested a conception of growth which features the idea of *developmental tasks*. A list of these tasks is presented in Chapter 4. In order to interpret them properly, you should understand the rationale behind the theory. In the spaces below define and explain what Havighurst means by a developmental task and note how you might make use of these tasks in attempting to understand the behavior of your students.

Definition of a developmental task

_____

_____

_____

_____

_____

Explanation of use of developmental tasks to understand behavior

_____

_____

_____

_____

_____

2. The theories of Sigmund Freud are endorsed by many psychologists. The idea that a child may become *fixated* is a key aspect of Freudian theory. In the spaces below explain what Freud meant by fixation, then comment on the significance some psychologists attribute to this concept. Finally, note some general criticisms which have been made of Freudian theory and summarize the alternate theory of development proposed by John E. Anderson.

Explanation and example of fixation

_____

_____

_____

_____

_____

Wider implications of the concept of fixation

_____

_____

_____

_____

_____

Criticisms of Freudian theory and the alternate theory proposed by John E. Anderson

_____

_____

_____

_____

_____

_____

_____

_____

3. At the present time the Gesell Institute readiness tests are being widely used. They are based on a theory of development put forward by Arnold Gesell. To understand the tests (and their possible limitations), you should be able to give a brief outline of Gesell's theory. And to make inferences about the validity of the tests, you should be able to cite some of the criticisms which have been leveled at Gesell's work. In the spaces below provide information relating to these two points.

Description of the basic idea of Gesell's theory

_____

_____

_____

_____

_____

Criticisms of Gesell's work

_____

_____

_____

_____

_____

_____

_____

4. Jean Piaget's analysis of the stages of intellectual development represents the most important single set of age-level descriptions presented in Chapter 4. In order to comprehend these stages satisfactorily, you should know something about Piaget's background and the general approach he took in making observations and building his theory. You should also have at least a general idea of what he means by four of his basic principles: *organization, adaptation, assimilation,* and *accommodation.* In the spaces below comment on each of these aspects of Piaget's theory.

Piaget's background

_____

_____

_____

_____

_____

Approach taken by Piaget in making observations and building his theory

_____

_____

_____

_____

_____

_____

Brief explanation of four key Piaget principles:

Organization

_____

_____

_____

Adaptation

_____

_____

_____

Assimilation

_____

_____

_____

Accommodation

_____

_____

_____

Suggestions for Further Reading, Thinking, and Discussion

3–1   Looking for Literal Examples of Overlap

A factor that complicates the prediction of student behavior on the basis of age-level characteristics is *overlap*. To become aware of how and why this is so, consider performing this simple study: Station yourself outside a public school toward the end of the day and observe students as they emerge from different classrooms. Those who come out of each room will usually be the same chronological age. First, note the range of sizes and shapes within a given group. Then as the children begin to mix in the hall or school grounds, see if you can clearly identify those who belong to the same age group. If you make such a survey, report your results and comment on their implications.

3–2   Becoming Aware of the Complications of Actuarial Prediction

Scientists try to predict behavior so that it will be possible to control behavior. Knowing age-level characteristics permits teachers to forecast and thus control (or allow for) the behavior of their students. The predictions may have only limited value as the basis for uniformly successful pedagogical techniques, however, because of the nature of *group* or *actuarial* prediction. Individuals vary tremendously, and there are exceptions to any rule. To get an idea of the range of individual differences to be found in practically any classroom, obtain permission to observe in a class at the grade level you expect to teach. Pick out two students who strike you as being at opposite extremes with regard to one or more qualities you select (e.g., energy, self-confidence, physical size, attractiveness). Observe each one for five or ten minutes (more, if you can) and write a brief personality sketch of each student. Then compare your two sketches. Do they seem to be describing students who are essentially the same or noticeably different? Comment on the implications of your findings.

3–3   Checking on the Predictability and Uniformity of Behavior at Different Age Levels

One of the principles mentioned in Chapter 3 is that the pattern of development becomes less predictable with increasing age. To check on the applicability of this principle, make arrangements to observe in a nursery school (with children of approximately the same chronological age) and a high school class. Note behavior which seems typical of each group. You might concentrate on such things as coordination, size, or impression of general maturity. Do you detect greater variability in the younger or the older students? Write your reactions and comment on the implications of your observations.

3–4   Observing Development from General to Specific Responses

Another principle noted in Chapter 3 is that development proceeds from general to specific responses. To check on the applicability of this principle, make arrangements to observe in an elementary school. Start in the kindergarten, paying special attention to how well the children are able to manipulate small objects such as pencils and scissors. Then go to a third grade and finally a sixth grade. (If this is not possible, observe children from different grade levels at play during recess.) Do the older students seem to have greater control over their fine muscles? Note your reactions and comment on the implication of your observations.

3–5   Checking on Irregularities in Growth

Still another principle mentioned in Chapter 3 is that although long-term growth is continuous, short-term growth may be irregular. To check on the applicability of this principle, obtain permission to interview an elementary school teacher and ask her whether she notices occasional backsliding in her pupils. Write down any specific examples she gives, and then comment on the implications of such regressions in behavior.

3–6   Taking a Closer Look at Havighurst's Developmental Tasks

Since the descriptions of developmental tasks in the lists of age-level characteristics are brief and incomplete, you may want to read sections of the complete list in Havighurst's *Developmental Tasks and Education* (1952). In the first chapter ("Life and Learning") and the fourth chapter ("Characteristics of Developmental Tasks") Havighurst provides the general theory behind the concept. The remaining six chapters discuss tasks for various levels of development. Read Chapters 1 and 4 and the chapter covering the tasks for the grade level that you expect to teach, and then note your reactions to what you have read.

3–7   Checking on the Stages of Development Described
by the Gesell Institute

If you would like more information about the basic beliefs of the Gesell Institute, read *The Gesell Institute's Child Behavior* (1955) by Frances Ilg and Louise Bates Ames. Its opening chapter presents an overview of the developmental theory endorsed by the Institute. On page 22 is a table illustrating the basic conception that children go through a series of highly predictable stages (due to the influence of universal, inborn factors). You might look at this table and then either observe children you know are of a given chronological age or interview teachers or parents. See if you can find consistent evidence to substantiate the suggestion of the Institute that behavior follows a highly predictable pattern. (On pages 22 through 24 Ilg and Ames explain why the pattern might *not* appear in all children. If you fail to find clear-cut trends, read this explanation and ask yourself whether you are satisfied with it. If you are not, consider the problem of allowing for overlap in interpreting developmental changes, which are said to occur at six-month intervals.) Comment on the results of your observations or interviews and note implications to be drawn from the results.

An alternate source of information about the Gesell Institute theory is *School Readiness* (1965), also by Ilg and Ames. Its first chapter presents the authors' point of view and includes suggestions for grouping pupils on the basis of performance on the Gesell Institute readiness tests. (A brief outline of the tests begins on page 35.) Read the opening chapter of this book, glance at the description of the tests, and record your reactions. Are you willing to place complete faith in the Gesell theory? Do you detect any limitations in the theory or in the tests? (For example, do you think the test questions are "fair" for children with underprivileged backgrounds? Ilg and Ames claim that a child cannot be coached on the items. Do you agree?)

3–8   Relating the Observations of Lorenz to Human Behavior

No less an authority than Julian Huxley has called Konrad Lorenz "one of the outstanding naturalists of our day." In *King Solomon's Ring* (1952) Lorenz describes many of his early observations and experiments with animals, including his first observations of *imprinting*. (You will find it at the beginning of Chapter 5, "Laughing at Animals.") Almost any part of this book is enjoyable and instructive, but Chapter 8 ("The Language of Animals") and Chapter 11 ("Morals and Weapons") are especially interesting. The latter chapter examines a theme which is developed more completely in *On Aggression* (1966)—about the nature of aggression in animal and man. Sample Chapter 3 ("What Aggression Is Good For"), Chapter 13 ("Ecce Homo!"), or Chapter 14 ("Avowal of Optimism"). If you read any sections of either of these books, briefly record your reactions—with emphasis on how they relate to education and our society.

3–9   Sampling Hunt's Views on "Intelligence and Experience"

James McVicker Hunt is perhaps the leading advocate of the hypothesis that enriched stimulation during critical periods produces sizable increments in intelligence. To sample Hunt's defense of the hypothesis, look for *Intelligence and Experience* (1961). Many parts of this book are quite technical, but you will find a summary in Chapter 9. (Chapter 8 presents "Some Reinterpretations" of studies relating to the impact of heredity and environment on intelligence—from the viewpoint of the current leading spokesman for environmentalists.) If you read either chapter, summarize the arguments presented and note your own reactions.

3–10 Sampling Bloom's Observations on Stability and Change in Human Characteristics

The "bible" of many advocates of early-childhood education is Benjamin Bloom's *Stability and Change in Human Characteristics* (1964). If you are curious as to how Bloom arrived at his estimate that 50 percent of adult intelligence is achieved by the age of four and 80 percent by the age of eight, peruse this book, paying special attention to Chapters 1, 3, 6, and 7. Are you convinced that these estimates are reasonable, well established, and valid? Speculate too about Bloom's hypothesis that I.Q. "losses" early in life are irreversible. For example, do you think a child who has had a relatively unstimulating preschool environment will fail to respond if he encounters an enthusiastic and effective first-grade teacher? (Think of a child who stays home and plays with toys in the backyard as compared to one who goes to nursery school, rather than of a child who is *deprived* of almost all stimulation.) If you follow up on either or both of these suggestions, write a brief summary of your reactions.

3–11 Reading about the Education of the Wild Boy of Aveyron

Jean Marc Itard (1775–1838) was a physician who became intrigued with the possibility of "humanizing" a feral child discovered in the company of a pack of wolves in a forest in the Aveyron region of France. He spent five years attempting to convert the wolf-child into a young man. His efforts were hampered by the fact that the boy's sight and hearing were severely impaired, but Itard's experiences make a fascinating story, reported in *The Wild Boy of Aveyron*. If you would like to gain some insight into how Itard set about his task, you are urged to browse through this book and summarize your reactions. Keep in mind that Itard based his methods on only limited data about behavior and learning. In the 170 years since he worked with Victor (the wolf-boy), a great deal of information which was not available to Itard has been discovered and tested. In later chapters of the text, different educators' techniques for working with deprived and retarded children will be discussed. At this point you might describe how *you* would approach the job if you were asked to educate a nine-year-old boy found leading a pack of wolves in Yellowstone Park.

3–12 Discovering More about the Montessori Method

Maria Montessori was a remarkable woman. The first woman to earn an M.D. degree in Italy and an energetic and imaginative innovator, she was much influenced by the work of Itard (and of Edouard Seguin), particularly his attempts to develop the sensory capacities of Victor. Although she originally applied Itard's techniques to the education of the retarded, she eventually turned to the teaching of preschool children. You can read Montessori's own descriptions of how she approached this task in *The Montessori Method, Dr. Montessori's Own Handbook,* or *Spontaneous Activity in Education.* These books not only are of interest because of the way they are written (which reveals the "character" of Maria Montessori), but provide all sorts of ideas which can be used with present-day American children. If you sample sections of any of these books, note your general reactions and comment on suggestions made by Montessori which strike you as most promising for use in nursery schools and kindergartens in the United States of the 1970's.

3–13   Gaining Fuller Understanding of Piaget's Theory

Since Jean Piaget is mentioned so frequently in the text, you may wish to learn more about the views of this famous Swiss psychologist. For a detailed description of his theory of intellectual development, consult *The Developmental Psychology of Jean Piaget* (1963) by John Flavell or *Piaget's Theory of Intellectual Development: An Introduction* (1969) by Herbert Ginsburg and Sylvia Opper. The latter book has a biography of Piaget in the opening chapter and a concise summary of the theory together with speculations on its pedagogical significance in the final chapter. You might skim through either of these books and pick out and comment on sections which are appropriate to the grade level of the students you will teach or sections which strike you as worthy of note.

3–14   Reading an Autobiographical Sketch of Gesell or Piaget

Autobiographical sketches written by famed psychologists Arnold Gesell and Jean Piaget are to be found in Volume IV (1952) of *A History of Psychology in Autobiography* edited by Edwin G. Boring and others. If you are interested enough to read either of these sketches, try to relate the background of the man to the Zeitgeist of the times and to trace possible influences which led him to develop his theory.

Age-Level Characteristics

Key Points

Facts

First large-muscle control, then small-muscle control
Soft skull bones in primary-grade children
Full accommodation of eyes at age 8
Average age of puberty: 12.5 for girls, 14 for boys

**Sequences
and Trends**

Faster maturation in girls than in boys
Growth spurt toward end of elementary school years
Egocentric speech, socialized speech (Piaget)
Moral realism, moral relativism (Piaget)
Intellectual development: sensorimotor, preoperational, concrete operations, and
   formal operations (Piaget)
Enactive, iconic, and symbolic thought (Bruner)
Developmental tasks (Havighurst)

Experiments

Mere verbal learning from "mastering" conservation principle early (Smedslund)
Age as best predictor of ability to conserve, but lag in disadvantaged (Almy)
Cheating by all children when stakes sufficiently high (Hartshorne and May)

Principles

Conservation, decentration, reversibility (Piaget)

Methodology

Obtaining, recording, and interpreting sociometric data
Applying guidelines of Almy and of Piaget (stages of intellectual development)

Chapter Contents

Testing and Organizing Your Knowledge of Key Points in Chapter 4

Facts

Chapter 4 presented a number of facts regarding age-level characteristics, familiarity with which can help you understand behavior or assist your students in a variety of ways. A selection of facts relating to different phases of development follows. You are asked to offer some comments which indicate your awareness of the possible significance to a teacher of each bit of information noted.

Girls (on the average) mature more rapidly than boys. How might this difference in development rate affect student learning, attitudes, and behavior?

_____

_____

_____

_____

_____

Large-muscle control precedes small-muscle control. How might teachers take this fact into account in arranging classroom activities at the lower grade levels?

_____

_____

_____

_____

The bones of younger children are relatively soft, including bones in the skull. Explain why teachers should not only keep this condition in mind themselves but also alert students to it.

_____

_____

_____

_____

The eyes of primary-grade children may not have matured to the point where they fully accommodate. Comment on what a teacher might do in allowing for this limitation.

_____

_____

_____

_____

The average age of puberty is twelve and a half for girls, fourteen for boys. What is the significance of the development of sexual maturity and how might teachers assist students to adjust to this important stage of maturation?

_____

_____

_____

_____

Sequences and Trends

1. Physical growth (as reflected by height and weight) follows a relatively continuous and steady pattern (in keeping with a principle of growth noted in Chapter 3). However, a marked growth spurt occurs in the otherwise smooth physical development of most children. Since this spurt represents a rather abrupt and unexpected departure from the normal rate, it often is a cause of concern for children at the time they experience it. You should therefore have some understanding of the nature of the growth spurt. In the spaces below comment on the timing of the growth spurt, explain how the more rapid maturation of girls (which causes them to experience it earlier than boys) may lead to difficulties, indicate why fast-maturing girls and slow-maturing boys may be especially upset by the timing of the spurt, and mention some ways teachers might lend sympathy and moral support to students who are notably bothered by their sudden or ill-timed spurt of growth.

Timing of growth spurt

_____

_____

_____

_____

Why earlier maturation of girls may cause difficulties

_____

_____

_____

_____

_____

Why fast-maturing girls and slow-maturing boys may be especially upset

_____

_____

_____

_____

_____

_____

How you might offer sympathy and support

_____

_____

_____

_____

_____

_____

_____

2. In Chapter 3 you were asked to consider the basic distinction Jean Piaget makes between *egocentric* and *socialized* speech. In Chapter 4 you were acquainted with the possible pedagogical significance of this distinction. Comment below on the problems a teacher may encounter in allowing for differences between egocentric and socialized speech as manifested in class recitation, and note some techniques for dealing with "irrelevant" (essentially egocentric) remarks made by students.

Problems which might be caused by egocentric speech

_____

_____

_____

_____

_____

_____

Techniques for dealing with egocentric recitation

_____

_____

_____

_____

_____

_____

_____

3. In Chapter 3 you were asked to consider the distinction Piaget makes between *moral realism* and *moral relativism*. In the spaces below explain some of the problems which stem from students' functioning as moral realists, note techniques a teacher might use in allowing for these, and comment on how moral relativism might be encouraged.

Problems stemming from students' functioning as moral realists

_____

_____

_____

_____

_____

How a teacher might allow for moral realism and encourage moral relativism

_____

_____

_____

_____

_____

_____

4. In Chapter 3 you were asked to indicate your familiarity with Piaget's four stages of intellectual development and with Jerome Bruner's three stages of thought. In Chapter 4 you were acquainted with the possible pedagogical significance of these two sequences. For the particular grade level you expect to teach, outline the characteristics of the appropriate stage of intellectual development as described by Piaget and Bruner, then explain how you might allow for these characteristics in your teaching.

Characteristics of appropriate stage of development described by Piaget

_____

_____

_____

_____

_____

_____

Characteristics of appropriate stage of development described by Bruner

_____

_____

_____

_____

_____

_____

_____

How you might allow for these characteristics in your teaching

_____

_____

_____

_____

_____

_____

_____

_____

5. In Chapter 3 you were asked to indicate your awareness of what Robert Havighurst means by *developmental tasks*. Chapter 4 provided lists of these tasks arranged by types of behavior and age levels. For the particular grade level you expect to teach, record three of the developmental tasks described by Havighurst.

Three developmental tasks appropriate for students at the grade level you expect to teach

a. _____

_____

_____

b. _____

_____

_____

c. _____

_____

_____

Experiments

1. Jean Piaget has reported that he is almost invariably asked the "American question" when he addresses educators in this country. Americans want to know whether the rate at which children proceed through the stages of intellectual development can be speeded up. A number of experiments have been conducted to check on this possibility. The studies of Jan Smedslund and those of Millie Almy have served as models for others to follow. Since these experiments are so highly regarded and since "the American question" is an important one, you should be familiar with the results reported by Smedslund and Almy. In the spaces below describe the experimental design and findings of the Smedslund studies on the impact of training intended to speed up understanding of the conservation concept. Then note some implications of the results of these experiments.

Design and results of the Smedslund experiments

_____

_____

_____

_____

_____

_____

_____

Implications of the results

_____

_____

_____

_____

In the spaces below summarize the nature and conclusions of the studies conducted by Almy and her associates on training for mastery of the conservation concept. Then comment on the implications of the conclusions, first in terms of how they relate to Piaget's philosophy of education and second in terms of the possible impact of a disadvantaged background on intellectual development.

Nature and conclusions of experiments conducted by Almy

_____

_____

_____

_____

_____

_____

How Almy's conclusions relate to Piaget's philosophy of education

_____

_____

_____

_____

_____

_____

How Almy's conclusions relate to the impact of a disadvantaged background

_____

_____

_____

_____

_____

_____

2. Hartshorne and May conducted a classic study of honesty. Since many pupils are likely to feel pressured to cheat at some point in their academic careers, knowledge of the results of this study may help you anticipate and minimize cheating. In the space below describe the general findings reported by Hartshorne and May and then comment on how these might be taken into account to reduce pressures to cheat.

Results of Hartshorne and May investigation

_____

_____

_____

How these results might be taken into account in minimizing cheating

_____

_____

_____

_____

_____

Principles

Conservation, decentration, and *reversibility* are three basic principles of Piaget's theory of intellectual development which are especially important to teachers who wish to analyze their students' thinking. If you are to benefit from the observations of Piaget, you should be able to describe what he means by each of these principles. In the spaces below give a succinct explanation.

Conservation

_____

_____

_____

Decentration

_____

_____

_____

Reversibility

_____

_____

_____

Methodology

1. The results of her studies prompted Millie Almy to offer some suggestions to those who wish to teach in accordance with Piaget's theories. While her proposals apply most directly to the elementary level, with slight adjustments they can also be used at any other level of school. In the space below note two of Almy's general guidelines for those who would like to teach in a manner in harmony with Piaget's theory of intellectual development.

a. _____

_____

_____

_____

_____

b. _____

_____

_____

_____

_____

2. Sociometric techniques provide a means for discovering students' social preferences. If you will be teaching at the elementary level, you may wish to obtain sociometric responses from your pupils. In the spaces below describe how you might ask pupils to give such responses, how the responses could be recorded on a target diagram, and how special attention might be paid to *stars* and *isolates*.

How you would ask students to give sociometric responses

_____

_____

_____

_____

How you would record responses on a target diagram

_____

_____

_____

_____

How you would take into account stars and isolates

_____

_____

_____

_____

_____

_____

Suggestions for Further Reading, Thinking, and Discussion

4-1 Comparing Real Students with Hypothetical Students

For the various reasons given in analyzing potential weaknesses of age-level characteristic descriptions, any discussion of developmental trends is bound to be somewhat inaccurate. Consequently, you might find it of interest to observe students at the grade level you propose to teach and compare what you see with the descriptions that have been provided. If possible, observe students in and out of class and then reread the appropriate set of descriptions for that grade level. What bits of behavior fit the descriptions, and what episodes or characteristics are contradictory? Pick out the _single_ characteristic which impresses you the most and speculate about what you might do—if anything—to allow for it when you begin to teach.

4-2 Using Havighurst's Developmental Tasks to Assess Maturity

At the conclusion of most sections on age-level characteristics in Chapter 4, some developmental tasks of Robert Havighurst are listed. You will gain deeper understanding of this concept by compiling a set of the developmental tasks for the grade level you expect to be dealing with and then observing the behavior of pupils with reference to it. Obtain permission to observe in a classroom at an appropriate grade level. Pick out at least two students who seem to have mastered most of the developmental tasks and two students who seem to have failed to master them. Do the students who have completed the tasks appear to be happier and more successful than those who have not? Check on your quick "intuitive" impression by asking the teacher about the performance and adjustment of the pupils you have selected. (Note: If you are intrigued by the concept of developmental tasks and impressed with the potential value of making observations with reference to these descriptions, obtain a copy of Havighurst's _Human Development and Education_ [1953]. This is an enlarged revision of the concise paperback *Developmental Tasks and Education* [1952]. It presents a fuller explanation of the tasks and includes rating scales for estimating the completion of the tasks at ages ten, thirteen, and sixteen.)

4–3   Trying Out a Piaget Experiment

One of the best ways to assess a student's level of intellectual development (and to learn a great deal about the theories of Jean Piaget) is to perform one of the experiments of Piaget (or his followers). At the primary level, you might use the beaker or clay experiments; at the upper elementary or junior high school level, the pendulum problem. Detailed descriptions of these and many other experiments performed by Piaget appear in Chapters 3 and 4 of *Piaget's Theory of Intellectual Development* (1969) by Herbert Ginsburg and Sylvia Opper. If you will be teaching at the primary-grade level, you might also consult *Young Children's Thinking* (1966) by Millie Almy, E. Chittenden, and P. Miller. In case you do try out a Piaget experiment, note the results and your own reactions, including any insight you gained into how the mind of a child or an adolescent works. (It would be interesting to compare your own results with those of classmates who tried the experiment on other children.)

4–4   Checking on Understanding of Abstract Concepts

If you do not have time to perform one of Piaget's experiments, you might use a simpler technique to get insight into the thought processes of a child. Ask a teacher at almost any level beyond the primary grades to have the students write out the Pledge of Allegiance to the flag and then *explain* it; e.g., what is the meaning of *allegiance, republic, indivisible, liberty, justice?* Analyze the results, write an evaluation of how well the students really understand what they are saying, compare your evaluation to Piaget's outline of the stages of intellectual development, and comment on the implications. (For example, how many students seem to have reached the stage of *formal* operations?)

4–5   Checking on Moral Realism and Moral Relativism

Piaget has suggested that children tend to be *moral realists* until about the end of the elementary school years, at which point they become *moral relativists*. For insight into this distinction, obtain permission to ask pupils at lower and upper grades in an elementary school to explain how they would react to these situations:

a. Suppose your mother bought a new dress. She was very proud of it, but you thought it looked terrible. If she asked you what you thought about it, what would you say?

b. Suppose two boys stole candy bars in a supermarket. One boy had plenty of money to pay for them; the other came from a poor family, had no money, and was very hungry. Should both boys be punished in the same way if they are caught?

c. Suppose John was playing ball on the playground and accidentally hit Mary and gave her a bloody nose. During the same recess period David got mad at Jane and hit her. It hurt, but it wasn't nearly as bad as Mary's bloody nose. John caused greater injury to Mary than David did to Jane. Does this mean John should be punished more severely than David?

According to Piaget, younger children are more likely to apply the letter of the law (*never* tell a lie) than the spirit of the law (it is all right to tell a "white lie"); less likely to take into account circumstances (such as hunger and poverty); and more likely to judge the seriousness of an act by its practical consequences rather than the intent of the individual (a child who causes a more serious injury should be more severely punished even if he did it accidentally). Did the responses from younger and older students fit these predictions? Summarize and comment on your results.

4–6 Assessing Feelings about Cheating

Because of various pressures to get high grades, many if not most students are tempted to cheat. For insight into how your pupils will react to pressures to do well in school, obtain permission to interview students at the grade level you hope to teach. With younger pupils, you might simply ask whether they think it is wrong to cheat, and what a teacher should do if she catches someone cheating. Older students might be asked to write out their thoughts on the same general questions, and on what teachers might do to cut down or limit cheating. Summarize any general trends which emerge from the replies, and comment on the implications.

4–7 Looking for Examples of Egocentric Recitation

According to Piaget, a child's speech is primarily egocentric or self-centered until he reaches the age of seven or eight. Controlled observations of this hypothesis have led to the conclusion that the differentiation between egocentric and socialized speech is not as clear-cut as Piaget originally suggested. However, younger children do seem to have more difficulty taking into account the views expressed by their fellow students during class recitation. If you have the opportunity to observe in an elementary school classroom during a discussion period, replicate the observational study conducted by H. V. Baker— that is, classify the contributions made by different students under the following headings:

New topic not obviously related to what an earlier speaker said

New topic but apparently suggested by something said by a previous contributor

Logical continuation of a topic previously introduced

Describe your results and comment on their implications. (Note: You might try a similar analysis in a high school or college class to discover whether more mature students are always able to continue logically a topic previously introduced. If quite a few students do not do this, what are some possible explanations for "disorganized" recitation? What techniques might you use to make discussions flow more smoothly? Would you be inclined to either gently criticize or ignore irrelevant contributions, for example?)

4–8 Recording the Activities of an "Inactive" Student

When children enter school, they are required to learn to live with the inevitable restrictions imposed by the demands of group interaction. For example, they must learn that thirty-five children cannot speak at once, that they have to remain relatively quiet at certain times, that they must sit more or less in one place during formal or semiformal presentations or study periods. Many elementary students have a hard time controlling their natural inclinations to move about. To check on this problem—and at the same time gain insight into why the noise and activity level is high in elementary classrooms—obtain permission to observe in an elementary school. Pick out two or three pupils, observe each one for three to five minutes, and try to write down everything they do at a time when they are ostensibly "inactive," e.g., working on a written assignment, watching the teacher. (Make your record as unobtrusively as possible. Some college students who got carried away by this project found themselves being mimicked by half a roomful of elementary pupils—all of them taking notes on the college student taking notes on them.) If you perform this assignment, summarize and comment on your findings.

4–9 Analyzing the Hypothesis That American Males Are Feminized

A number of observers have suggested that one reason males in the United States have a higher suicide rate, a lower life expectancy, and more problems of many kinds than females is feminization early in life. Patricia Sexton has written at length about this hypothesis in *The Feminized Male* (1969). (An abridged version of her arguments can be found in an article in the January, 1970, issue of *Psychology Today* starting on page 23.) If you have ever speculated about this question, you might read either the book or the article, summarize Sexton's arguments, and record your own reactions.

4–10　Obtaining and Analyzing Sociometric Data

If you have the opportunity to observe or work with an elementary class for a period of several weeks, ask the teacher for permission to obtain some sociometric responses from the pupils. At the end of a written assignment, have students write down the name of the person they most like to work with. Before recording the responses on a target diagram, make your own estimate as to who the stars and isolates will be and request the teacher to do the same. (If you know the children well, you might even try to guess the choices each pupil will make.) Then compare your guesses with the actual results. Time permitting, repeat the request for sociometric responses a month later and check on the consistency of choices. Comment on your findings and speculate on what you might do with the sociometric information that you have obtained.

4–11　Reading and Reacting to a Book on Adolescence

In many respects, the most difficult and complex stage of development is adolescence. Countless books have been written on the problems young people face (and create) in our society, and every high school teacher should find it of interest to read one or more analyses of this phase of development. Paul Goodman has written two provocative books on the subject. In *Growing Up Absurd* (1956), he argues that growing up in America is literally an "absurdity." In *Compulsory Miseducation* (1964) he presents a critique of high school education in Part 2 and an evaluation of college education in Part 3. In Chapter 10 he puts forward "Two Simple Proposals" for reforming the systems.

Edgar Z. Friedenberg has also written two books on adolescence. In *The Vanishing Adolescent* (1959) he asserts that adolescence *is* conflict, that conflict is necessary for the young person to discover self-definition, and that lack of conflict in the lives of American youth means that adolescence has "vanished." (If you read this book, ask yourself whether there is more conflict now than there was in 1959 when the book was published.) In *Coming of Age in America* (1965), Friedenberg compares adolescents in the United States to those in African countries which have been colonized (Chapter 1), describes his perceptions of a "typical" American high school (Chapter 2), gives a description of student values (Chapter 3), and analyzes the shortcomings of educational practice (Chapter 4). In the concluding section of Chapter 6 he offers some prescriptions. (Among other things he suggests that most young teachers enter the field because they see teaching as "the easiest of professions" and that the selection of credential candidates must be upgraded.)

Note your reactions to whatever parts of these books you read.

4–12   Sampling Erikson's Views on Identity

Erik H. Erikson is a highly respected psychoanalyst who has specialized in observing human development. One of his most recent books is *Identity: Youth and Crisis* (1968). If you will be teaching in high school, and/or if you have ever been troubled in your own search for identity, you may find this book highly thought-provoking. Be warned, however, that Erikson addresses his remarks primarily to fellow clinicians and professionals of the older generation. The person under thirty may have to curb a tendency to be defensive over descriptions of youthful foibles which happen to coincide with aspects of his own behavior. While Erikson does not ridicule the behavior of young people, he does have an incisive way of describing it. To discover whether you are able to weigh his observations without feeling that you are being attacked, read Chapter 1, which provides an excellent summary of his views on identity.

Erikson has also written two biographies analyzing (among other things) the identity crisis of his subjects with reference to the Zeitgeist of the times. (These are in-depth variations of what Edwin G. Boring has done in his *History of Experimental Psychology*.) The biographies are of two extremely different individuals: Martin Luther and Mahatma Gandhi. If you enjoy biographies, or have ever wondered about the lives and times of Luther or Gandhi, look for *Young Man Luther* (1958) or *Gandhi's Truth* (1969). If you sample any of Erikson's works, summarize his views and add your own observations.

Part Three / Learning

Two Views of the Learning Process

	Key Points
Classifications	Impulsive and reflective thinkers, analytic and thematic thinkers (Kagan)
Experiments	Conditioning of dog to salivate when bell rings (Pavlov) Opening of latch by cat through trial and error (Thorndike) Shaping of behavior of rat and pigeon by reinforcement (Skinner) Solving of stick problem by ape through insight (Köhler)
Concepts	Emitted behavior, elicited behavior Classical conditioning, operant conditioning Terminal behavior, contingencies of reinforcement Life space (Lewin)
Principles	Reinforcement, extinction, generalization, discrimination Closure
Theories	Skinner's version of S-R associationism Bruner's version of cognitive-field theory
Methodology	Using programmed techniques: shaping behavior, vanishing prompts, using linear and branching programs, considering lowest-common-denominator effect Using the discovery approach: emphasizing contrast, stimulating informed guessing, introducing disturbing data, permitting mistakes

Chapter Contents

Testing and Organizing Your Knowledge of Key Points in Chapter 5

Classifications

Jerome Kagan has done considerable research on styles of thinking. He has found that it is often possible to identify *impulsive* and *reflective* thinkers and that some students seem to be primarily *analytic,* others *thematic.* When dichotomies of behavior are described, it often turns out upon further study that few people are *pure* examples of either type. Even though most people lean toward one form of behavior or the other, an individual is rarely completely consistent in all situations. If you guard against the tendency to classify all your students into one of Kagan's categories *or* the other, awareness that a given pupil is mainly impulsive or thematic or whatever may help you understand his behavior. In the spaces below describe each of the thinkers identified by Kagan and after each description comment on how knowledge of these types might be of value in understanding student behavior. (What techniques might you use in assisting a student to compensate for his natural tendency to be a certain type of thinker if it is causing problems in learning?)

Impulsive

_____

_____

_____

_____

_____

Reflective

_____

_____

_____

_____

Analytic

_____

_____

_____

_____

Thematic

_____

_____

_____

_____

Experiments

Chapter 2 briefly described four classic experiments in psychology: those conducted by Ivan Pavlov, Edward L. Thorndike, B. F. Skinner, and Wolfgang Köhler. The evidence yielded by these experiments led to the development of S-R associationism and cognitive-field theory, which in turn led to programmed instruction and the discovery approach. Because they are the basis for the two methods of teaching featured in Chapter 5, the experiments are discussed in greater detail in the opening sections of each half of the chapter. It will be to your advantage to become familiar with the techniques used by each man and to be able to relate their findings to programmed instruction or the discovery approach.

In the space below tell how Pavlov conditioned a dog to salivate when a bell rang and how this experiment became the basis for S-R associationism.

_____

_____

_____

_____

_____

_____

_____

In the space below explain how Thorndike studied learning in cats placed in puzzle boxes and how his experiments led to basic trends which have been stressed in most of the subsequent learning theories developed in the United States.

_____

_____

_____

_____

_____

_____

_____

_____

In the space below describe a typical Skinner-box experiment in which a rat is induced to push a bar under certain conditions, and also a typical Skinner experiment in which the behavior of a pigeon is shaped by reinforcement. Then explain how these simple experiments led to the development of programmed instruction.

_____

_____

_____

_____

_____

_____

_____

_____

_____

_____

In the space below describe the experiment of Wolfgang Köhler in which an ape was assisted to solve a problem by gaining insight. Explain how this experiment (and others like it) led to development of the discovery approach to learning.

_____

_____

_____

_____

_____

_____

_____

_____

_____

Concepts

1. At first glance, the experiments of Pavlov and Skinner may seem to be essentially the same. There are significant differences between them, however. A distinction is made between *elicited* behavior and *emitted* behavior, and the term *classical conditioning* is used to refer to Pavlov's kind of learning whereas *operant conditioning* refers to Skinner's kind of learning.

In the space below distinguish between elicited and emitted behavior and explain how this distinction highlights a basic difference between the Pavlov and Skinner experiments.

_____

_____

_____

_____

_____

_____

_____

_____

In the space below explain why Pavlov's type of conditioning is called *classical* and Skinner's version is called *operant*.

_____

_____

_____

_____

_____

_____

_____

2. Two key concepts of operant conditioning which are basic to techniques of programmed instruction are *terminal behavior* and *contingencies of reinforcement*. To understand why and how a program is written or how the principles of programmed instruction can be applied in the classroom, you should be able to explain what is meant by these two terms and how they fit into an

S-R associationist conception of learning. Write your explanations in the appropriate spaces below.

Terminal behavior

_____

_____

_____

_____

Contingencies of reinforcement

_____

_____

_____

_____

3. Kurt Lewin was a leading field theorist who was instrumental in arousing interest in Gestalt psychology in the United States. He developed the concept of the *life space,* which both exemplifies and illustrates key aspects of cognitive-field theory. In the spaces below draw a diagram of the life space of a high school girl who is ostensibly listening to a lecture on the War of 1812 but is actually dreaming about being crowned football queen. Then explain how the concept of the life space highlights a primary distinction between S-R associationism and cognitive-field theory.

Diagram of girl who dreams of being football queen

How the concept of the life space illustrates a distinction between S-R theory
and cognitive-field theory

_____

_____

_____

_____

_____

_____

_____

_____

_____

Principles

1. Although the experiments of Pavlov and Skinner differ in important
respects, they are similar in that both illustrate and establish some general
principles of learning. Since these principles are the basis for most variations
of S-R theory, including programmed instruction, you should be able to explain the nature of *reinforcement, extinction, generalization,* and *discrimination.* In the spaces below indicate how each of these principles is illustrated
by the experiments of Pavlov *and* Skinner and then note—in a general way—
how each might be applied to classroom practice. (For example, how might
you take into account the principle of reinforcement as you make plans for
interacting with your students?)

Reinforcement

_____

_____

_____

_____

_____

_____

_____

_____

Extinction

_____

_____

_____

_____

_____

_____

_____

_____

Generalization

_____

_____

_____

_____

_____

_____

_____

_____

_____

Discrimination

_____

_____

_____

_____

_____

_____

_____

_____

_____

_____

_____

2. Several principles resulted from the observations of behavior by early Gestalt psychologists. One of these—*closure*—is especially pertinent to understanding the reasoning behind the discovery approach. In the spaces below explain and give an example of the Gestalt principle of closure. Then note how awareness of this principle might assist you in setting up discovery sessions and in understanding and handling student reactions to classroom situations.

Explanation and example of closure

_____

_____

_____

_____

_____

_____

_____

_____

How awareness of closure might be of assistance to a classroom teacher

_____

_____

_____

_____

_____

_____

_____

_____

_____

Theories

The two basic theories of learning which are emphasized in the text are B. F. Skinner's interpretation of *S-R associationism* and Jerome S. Bruner's interpretation of *cognitive-field theory*. To comprehend the reasoning that led Skinner to develop programmed instruction and Bruner to develop his version of the discovery approach, you should be able to give a general statement of the theory behind each technique of teaching. In the following spaces record your capsule description of each theory.

Skinner's interpretation of S-R associationism

_____
_____
_____
_____
_____
_____

Bruner's interpretation of cognitive-field theory

_____
_____
_____
_____
_____
_____
_____

Methodology

1. *Programmed learning* was derived from applications of Skinner's interpretation of S-R associationism. The text suggests that you might write a program of your own, use a program written by someone else, or base your teaching techniques on the principles of programmed instruction. If you are to carry out these various suggestions in an informed way, you should be able to provide an example and/or explain something about the nature of each of the following techniques or concepts.

Shaping

_____
_____
_____
_____
_____
_____

Vanishing prompts

_____

_____

_____

_____

_____

_____

_____

_____

Linear and branching programs

_____

_____

_____

_____

_____

_____

_____

The lowest-common-denominator effect

_____

_____

_____

_____

_____

_____

_____

_____

2. The *discovery approach* is the basic method of teaching developed from cognitive-field theory. Specific discovery techniques suggested by Jerome S. Bruner and Morris Bigge include *emphasizing contrast, stimulating informed guessing, introducing disturbing data,* and *permitting mistakes.* Select *two* of these techniques and in the spaces below give an example of how each might be used (ideally with reference to a class *you* might teach) together with an explanation of how each exemplifies Gestalt principles.

a. _____

_____

_____

_____

_____

_____

b. _____

_____

_____

_____

_____

_____

Suggestions for Further Reading, Thinking, and Discussion

5–1   Sampling a Section of Skinner's "The Technology of Teaching"

The Technology of Teaching (1968) is B. F. Skinner's most concise and application-oriented discussion of operant conditioning techniques related to pedagogy. There are several sections of this book you might want to sample with the idea of eventually purchasing a copy for future reference. For an overview of programmed learning and teaching machines, see Chapter 3. In Chapter 5, "Why Teachers Fail," Skinner describes what he perceives to be common mistakes made by many teachers. Do you agree with his critique? In Chapter 8, "The Creative Student," he discusses determinism and the issue of personal freedom. Select one of these chapters, or another of your choice, and record your reactions to general or specific arguments made in the book.

5–2   Reacting to Some Dialogues with Skinner

In *B. F. Skinner: The Man and His Ideas* (1968), dialogues with Skinner (originally filmed for educational television) are recorded by Richard I. Evans. In Chapter 1 you will find "Reactions to Various Psychological Concepts," including the theories of Pavlov and Freud. Chapter 2, "Aversive Versus Positive Control of Behavior," comments on the incentive system in the Soviet Union and gives Skinner's reactions to criticisms of his Utopian novel *Walden Two.* Chapter 3, "The Formal Educational System," includes some of Skinner's observations on overconformity and the changing role of the American woman. If you are intrigued by Skinner and his theories, you may find it enjoyable to read and react to one or more of the dialogues recorded in this book.

(Note: Even though the books by Skinner and Huxley to be noted in exercises 5–3 and 5–4 were mentioned in the "Suggestions for Further Reading, Thinking, and Discussion" for Chapter 2, they are called to your attention once again on the assumption that information presented in Chapter 5 might have aroused more interest in applying learning theory to create a Utopia [or an anti-Utopia].)

5–3   Speculating about Skinner's Utopia

In *Walden Two* (1948), B. F. Skinner describes his conception of a Utopia based on the application of science to human behavior. To get the full impact of the novel and of Skinner's ideas, you should read the entire book. (As a matter of fact, it may be hard to put down once you begin it.) However, if you cannot read the whole thing at this time, Chapters 12 through 17—in which the approach to child rearing and education at Walden Two is described —may be of special interest to you as a future teacher. Start to read at page 95 and continue through at least page 148 to get a sample of life in Skinner's Utopia. Then record your reactions, including perhaps an opinion as to whether you might like to join a society based on the ideas of Walden Two. Take a stab too at sketching out a Utopia of your own—perhaps you will be able to come up with one that is an improvement over Skinner's version.

5–4   Considering Huxley's View of an Anti-Utopia

In *Brave New World* (1932), Aldous Huxley presented his conception of what might be characterized as an *anti*-Utopia founded on the principles of conditioning. While Skinner describes how such principles could be used to set man free, Huxley shows how they could be used to enslave man. If you read *Brave New World,* ask yourself whether any of the predictions Huxley made in 1932 have come true. (For example, is our behavior "conditioned" by TV commercials? How many people make habitual use of pain relievers or tranquilizers?) Then after you have arrived at some answers, record your thoughts in writing.

5–5   Making a First Effort at Writing a Program

In writing a program, you should start by getting some initial feedback from a sample of students. Select a concept from this course, or from a subject you will eventually teach, and write a ten-frame program, try it out on four or five classmates, and note their reactions. Even if the frames and reactions are not exactly the same as those you might eventually use with younger students, the feedback you get could help you sort out your thoughts regarding programmed instruction. For suggestions on how to write the program, look over a few actual programs or glance through *Good Frames and Bad: A Grammar of Frame Writing* (1964) by Susan Meyer Markle, *A Guide to Programed Instruction* (1963) by Jerome Lysaught and Clarence Williams, or *Practical Programing* (1966) by Peter Pipe.

5–6   Trying a Program Yourself and Recording Your Reactions

A good way to find out about a pedagogical technique is to try it yourself—from the *student* point of view. To clarify your thoughts about programmed instruction, record your reactions to any programmed books, units, or courses you have taken, or—if you have never been exposed to this technique—seek out a programmed unit and work through it. To find a suitable program, ask your instructor for assistance, check with classmates who have used one in the past, browse through a college bookstore, or consult with the person in charge of a curriculum and materials section of a library.

5–7   Sampling Bruner's "Toward a Theory of Instruction"

Toward a Theory of Instruction (1966) is Jerome Bruner's most concise and application-oriented book on teaching. Sampling a few sections of this book will help you decide whether to purchase a copy for future reference. Chapter 3, "Notes on a Theory of Instruction," provides an overview of Bruner's views on teaching and learning. Chapter 4 describes a course of study (of man) taught through the use of the discovery approach. You might read either or both of these chapters, or another section of your own choice, and record your reactions.

5–8   Pondering the Place of Fantasy and Feeling in Education

Richard M. Jones participated in the development of the discovery approach to teaching social studies which Bruner describes in *Toward a Theory of Instruction*. As Jones observed the experimental teaching sessions, he decided that Bruner had made an excellent start toward a theory of instruction but had not carried the technique to its logical conclusions. In *Fantasy and Feeling in*

Education (1968) Jones suggests that teachers do everything possible to enlist the "emotional and imaginal responses" of the child as he learns. He describes class sessions in which the Bruner materials were tried out and argues that the most meaningful learning took place when a situation of "controlled emotion" existed. If you will be teaching at the upper elementary level and are attracted by Bruner's approach to teaching the unit on Man (and/or if you hope to make learning a highly personal experience, regardless of grade level and subject matter), you will find *Fantasy and Feeling in Education* of interest. In Chapter 2 Jones explains the importance of controlled emotion, in Chapter 3 he develops the theme that affect and imagery are the skills most needed to teach social studies, and in Chapter 4 he makes a distinction between insight and *outsight*. Chapter 6 is devoted to a theoretical frame for considering emotional growth which is based on Erik H. Erikson's interpretation of Freudian theory, and in the remaining three chapters Jones presents his version of a more complete theory of instruction than that offered by Bruner and a description of how he feels Man: A Course of Study should be taught. If you read any of these chapters, note points which you feel will be of value when you begin to teach.

5–9   Writing a Description of a Discovery Unit

If the discovery approach strikes you as promising, briefly describe a unit you might eventually use in a class of your own which features one or more of the specific discovery techniques proposed by Bruner (emphasize contrast, stimulate informed guessing, encourage participation, stimulate awareness), Bigge (switch subject matter, introduce disturbing data, permit mistakes), or Davis (torpedoing). To get feedback, write a short description of a discovery unit and show the outline to some classmates for their reactions. Summarize their responses and add comments of your own.

5–10   Speculating about the Perceptual View of Behavior

In *Individual Behavior* (1959), Arthur Combs and Donald Snygg discourse extensively on their version of cognitive-field theory, which they call the perceptual approach to behavior. Part I of this book provides theoretical background; Part II consists in a discussion of implications and applications. As a future teacher, you will find chapters in the latter section particularly interesting. Chapter 15, "The Individual and His Society," presents a series of principles pertaining to individuals and their relationships to society. In Chapter 17 "The Goals and Purposes of Education" are discussed. Chapter 18 is devoted to "The Teaching Relationship." For additional information on the perceptual view, read one or more of these chapters (or another of your choice) and record your reactions.

5–11   Describing the Way Two Fanatics Might Approach the Teaching of Square Dancing

To point up the differences between programmed learning and the discovery approach, you might find it enjoyable to write a description of how square dancing, for example, could be taught by two extremists. First, tell how a person fanatically committed to S-R theory would set about the task. Then turn your imagination to how a true believer in the discovery approach might arrange things if he were asked to teach square dancing. (Any other idea or activity could be substituted for square dancing. The important thing is to let yourself go—write a wildly exaggerated account of how S-R principles and field theory might be used to the point of becoming ridiculous. In the process you may learn about both the strengths and weaknesses of each approach to learning.)

5–12   Reading and Reacting to Neill's "Summerhill"

If you have never read any of A. S. Neill's books on education and child rearing, you might want to do so before embarking on a teaching career. *Summerhill* (1960) is probably the most straightforward account of the school of that name, in which Neill has put his philosophy into practice for over forty years. You are urged to read the Foreword by Erich Fromm first. In the opening section of the book, Neill gives a complete, although somewhat disorganized, exposition of what the school is like. For a more complete and specific idea as to what actually takes place at Summerhill, browse through *Living at Summerhill* (1968) by Herb Snitzer. For opinions of some graduates of the school which will provide a frame of reference for sorting out your reactions, read "What Does a Summerhill Old School Tie Look Like?" by Emmanuel Bernstein in the January, 1968, issue of *Psychology Today*.

5–13   Reacting to Holt's Criticisms of American Education

John Holt has been one of the most outspoken critics of American education during the past decade, notably in *How Children Fail* (1964), *How Children Learn* (1967), and *The Underachieving School* (1969). Holt is a sensitive and perceptive observer, and you may endorse many of the points he makes regarding the shortcomings of traditional educational practice. As you read his prescriptions for reform, however, ask yourself about the feasibility and practicality of the alternatives he suggests. In Parts I and II of *How Children Fail,* Holt discusses the strategies children use to avoid a sense of failure and why they fear failure to such an extent. What might you do in your own classes to avoid the sorts of situations he describes? Part III of that book takes up "real learning" and offers some suggestions on the proper way to teach—ideas which are developed more completely in *How Children Learn.* If you feel somewhat bitter about your own school experiences, you may find yourself in sympathy with Holt's proposals for reform. But, in assessing them, try to come up with ideas of your own which are not as extreme (and are perhaps more realistic).

5–14   Reading an Autobiographical Sketch of a Learning Theorist

Now that you have read about learning theory, you may be inclined to read an autobiographical sketch of one of the theorists selected for inclusion in *A History of Psychology in Autobiography.* Sketches by Edward L. Thorndike and John B. Watson appear in Volume III (1936) edited by Carl Murchison. The sketch by B. F. Skinner appears in Volume V (1967) edited by Edwin G. Boring and Gardner Lindzey. If you read one of these autobiographies, speculate about how the impact of the Zeitgeist of the times and the background and experiences of the individual might have influenced his theory. (Note: Skinner describes his own perceptions of how he was operant-conditioned to perform in certain ways as he studied the experiments he was conducting on rats and pigeons in "A Case History in Scientific Method," which you will find in Volume II of *Psychology: A Study of Science, General Systematic Formulations, Learning and Special Processes,* edited by Sigmund Koch, pages 359–379.)

Teaching Different Types of Learning

Key Points

Sequences

Discovery stages: preparation, incubation, illumination, verification (Wallas)

Classifications

Types of learning: signal, stimulus-response, chaining, verbal associations, multiple discrimination, concepts, principles, problem solving (Gagné)

Taxonomy of educational objectives, cognitive domain (Bloom)

Concepts

Habitual set, functional fixedness

Methodology

Teaching verbal associations by using chaining, mediating links (mnemonic devices, advance organizers), and the progressive part method

Teaching concepts and principles by describing terminal behavior and then guiding learning step by step

Teaching problem solving by using techniques of Crutchfield, Suchman, and Bruner and by employing heuristics

Encouraging creativity by following the suggestions of Torrance

Chapter Contents

Testing and Organizing Your Knowledge of Key Points in Chapter 6

Sequences

A number of attempts to analyze the *process of discovery* have been made. One of the first theorists to study thought processes was G. Wallas. Knowledge of the stages proposed by Wallas as typical of the way a person makes a discovery not only renders the process understandable but may also allow you to help your students solve problems (and to analyze your own thinking). In the spaces below describe the four stages in the process of discovery as described by Wallas, and then give an example which illustrates the process.

Stages in the process of discovery as outlined by Wallas:

1. _____

2. _____

3. _____

4. _____

Example illustrating these stages in the process of discovery

_____
_____
_____
_____
_____
_____
_____
_____

Classifications

1. Robert Gagné has classified *conditions of learning* into eight basic types. Becoming familiar with this classification will assist you to set up learning experiences in a systematic and efficient way and make the most of the hierarchical aspects of many learning situations. You may also discover why some students have difficulty with higher-level learning: because they have not mastered lower-level "fundamentals." Gagné's eight types of learning are listed below. Give a brief explanation and an example of each.

Signal learning

_____
_____
_____
_____
_____

Stimulus-response learning

_____
_____
_____
_____
_____

Chaining

_____
_____
_____
_____
_____
_____

Verbal association

_____
_____
_____
_____
_____
_____

Multiple discrimination

_____
_____
_____
_____
_____
_____

Concept learning

_____
_____
_____
_____
_____
_____

Principle learning

_____
_____
_____
_____
_____
_____
_____

Problem solving

_____
_____
_____
_____
_____
_____

2. Benjamin Bloom and several associates have developed a *taxonomy of educational objectives* to help teachers organize learning experiences. (The way the Key Points for each chapter of the text are organized is an example of the use of the taxonomy.) Representing an alternative to Gagné's classification of types of learning, the taxonomy is quite complex, and since direct reference to it is necessary in order to use it, there is no point in memorizing it. However, you should be able to explain *why* the taxonomy was developed and *how* it might be used. Comment on these points in the spaces below.

Why taxonomy was developed

_____
_____
_____
_____
_____
_____

How taxonomy might be used

_____

_____

_____

_____

_____

_____

Concepts

The solving of problems is complicated by many limiting factors. Two specific characteristics of thinking which may prevent problem solving are *habitual set* and *functional fixedness*. If you remain aware of these two concepts, you may be able to assist your students to overcome certain mental blocks. In the spaces below explain and give an example of each concept, then note how you might help students deal with these blocks to learning.

Explanation and example of habitual set

_____

_____

_____

_____

_____

_____

Explanation and example of functional fixedness

_____

_____

_____

_____

_____

_____

Techniques for assisting students to overcome habitual set and functional fixedness

_____

_____

_____

_____

_____

_____

_____

_____

Methodology

1. In Gagné's classification of types of learning, *verbal associations* serve as a basis for the later mastery of concepts and principles. In helping students learn verbal associations, you may want to take into account *chaining,* the use of *mediating links* (such as *mnemonic devices* and *advance organizers*) and the *progressive part method.* In the spaces below explain and give an example of each of these techniques for assisting students to master verbal associations.

Explanation and example of chaining

_____

_____

_____

_____

_____

Explanation and example of a mnemonic device

_____

_____

_____

_____

Explanation and example of an advance organizer

_____

_____

_____

_____

_____

_____

Explanation and example of the progressive part method

_____

_____

_____

_____

_____

_____

2. After you have made sure your students know the necessary verbal associations and have taken steps to fill in gaps in their knowledge by using the above techniques, you will want to encourage them to learn and apply *concepts* and *principles*. Gagné suggests an approach which reflects an S-R interpretation of learning. That is, start out by describing the terminal behavior and then guide the learning so that students achieve this behavior step by step. In the space below explain how Gagné might assist students to understand and apply the principle of *conduction*. (You might start out with the statement "Let's figure out what happens when something made out of metal is heated.")

_____

_____

_____

_____

_____

_____

_____

3. Several theorists are currently stressing the importance of teaching problem solving or techniques of inquiry. Richard Crutchfield and his associates use a programmed approach. J. Richard Suchman and Jerome S. Bruner use discovery techniques. Gyorgy Polya emphasizes heuristics. In the spaces below describe how you might teach problem solving by methods similar to those of Crutchfield, Suchman and Bruner, and Polya.

Applying techniques developed by Crutchfield

_____

_____

_____

_____

_____

_____

Applying techniques developed by Suchman and Bruner

_____

_____

_____

_____

_____

_____

Applying techniques developed by Polya

_____

_____

_____

_____

_____

_____

_____

4. In addition to teaching approaches to problem solving, there is considerable interest at present in encouraging creativity (or avoiding squelching it). E. Paul Torrance has offered many suggestions on how this might be done. In the space below explain and illustrate five techniques (derived from Torrance's suggestions and/or based on observations made by Goertzel and Goertzel) for getting students to make the most of their creative potential.

a. _____

_____

_____

b. _____

_____

_____

c. _____

_____

_____

d. _____

_____

_____

e. _____

_____

_____

Suggestions for Further Reading, Thinking, and Discussion

6–1 Reading Gagné's Description of the Conditions of Learning

Gagné's book *The Conditions of Learning* (1965) gives the rationale behind his classification of learning (Chapters 1 and 2), explains each type of learning in detail (Chapters 3 through 6), and provides examples of how learning experiences might be guided in a systematic way by a sequence of lessons based on the classification. Gagné discusses learning structure in science instruction (starting on page 180), sequence in the learning of foreign languages (starting on page 190), and learning structure in English (starting

on page 196). Chapter 8 takes up motivation and transfer; Chapter 9 is devoted primarily to decisions on organizing learning experiences; media and
modes of instruction are analyzed in Chapter 10. If you like the idea of a carefully planned sequence of learning experiences, read one or more chapters of
The Conditions of Learning. Review Gagné's analysis in the sections you read
and comment on how you might use his suggestions in your own teaching.

6–2   Examining "Taxonomy of Educational Objectives: Cognitive Domain"

Chapter 6 of the text provides an abridged outline of the taxonomy developed by Benjamin Bloom and several associates published in *Taxonomy of
Educational Objectives: Cognitive Domain* (1956). To better understand the
taxonomy and to gain insight into coordinating objectives and evaluation,
examine this book. Chapter 1 describes "The Nature and Development of the
Taxonomy." Chapter 2 discusses "Educational Objectives and Curriculum
Development." The remainder of the book consists of definitions of the general and specific classifications followed by illustrations and exam questions.
As you take a closer look at the taxonomy, record possible ways in which you
might use it once you begin to teach.

6–3   Looking into the Productive-Thinking Program

Richard S. Crutchfield and his associates have developed a series of programmed picture-stories designed to "strengthen the elementary school student's ability to think." A discussion of the productive-thinking program appears in Chapter 4 ("Developing the Skills of Productive Thinking") of
Trends and Issues in Developmental Psychology (1969) edited by Paul H.
Mussen, Jonas Langer, and Martin Covington, and a curriculum library may
have a complete set of the materials used in the program. The sample illustrations shown on page 232 of the text may induce you to order your own set of
the lessons in the Productive Thinking Program. A set of sixteen lessons costs
$5.95 and can be obtained from Educational Innovation, Box 9428, Berkeley,
California, 94719. If you will be teaching at the upper elementary level, you
will probably find the Productive Thinking Program of considerable interest.
Lessons are in the form of illustrated stories which a student reads and re-
sponds to. If you have the opportunity to examine these materials, describe
your reactions to the program.

You might also consider using similar techniques to develop your own
productive-thinking program. One possibility would be to base individual or
class projects on comic books which present detective stories, perhaps even
those of Sherlock Holmes. For insight into how a master of detective fiction
provides the reader with all the clues before the detective solves the case, read

an Agatha Christie mystery featuring Hercule Poirot or Miss Marple. See if you can figure out the answer before the last chapter. All the clues will be at hand. If heuristics attracts you, read and try to solve a Poirot mystery on your own. Then read another and make full use of heuristics. Poirot does, and by employing "method" and his "little grey cells" he always manages to solve a case. You might even make certain Agatha Christie novels the basis for a productive-thinking program at the junior and senior high school levels.

6–4   Exploring Inquiry Training

J. Richard Suchman has sought the same goal as Crutchfield, i.e., fostering a student's ability to think or solve problems, but he favors a discovery rather than a programmed approach. To find out more about how Suchman institutes inquiry training (perhaps so that you can compare his method to that of Crutchfield) look for his book *The Elementary School Training Program in Scientific Inquiry* (1963) or an article, "Inquiry Training: Building Skills for Autonomous Discovery," which appeared in Volume 7, Number 3 (1961), of the *Merrill-Palmer Quarterly,* starting on page 147. If you read either of these, record your reactions and comment on how you might use techniques of inquiry training in your classes.

6–5   Reading about Bruner's Approach to Inquiry Training

Jerome S. Bruner's techniques of inquiry training are similar to, although somewhat less systematic than, Suchman's. You will find a description of how he encourages students to acquire general methods for solving problems in Chapter 3 of *Toward a Theory of Instruction* (1966). If you read this chapter, summarize your reactions to Bruner's approach and—if appropriate—tell how you might apply similar techniques in your classes.

(Note: Bruner uses exercises which are primarily mathematical. Suchman concentrates pretty much on phenomena of physical science. Crutchfield, on the other hand, features a variety of behavioral situations in his lessons. Thus Crutchfield's approach may be the most helpful to you in a wide range of situations.)

6–6   Reading and Reacting to Skinner's Criticisms of the Discovery Approach to Teaching Problem Solving

At various places in *The Technology of Teaching* (1968), B. F. Skinner criticizes the use of discovery techniques to teach inquiry or problem solving. He also offers arguments to support a programmed approach. One set of critical remarks starts on page 50 under the heading "Can Material Be Too Easy?"

Page 89 has it that "the teaching of truly creative behavior is . . . a contradiction in terms." Starting on page 131 is a section on "Solving Problems," followed by some observations on "Productive Thinking" (page 134), "Having Ideas" (page 139), and "The Role of the Thinker" (page 140). Chapter 8 is devoted to "The Creative Student." Let the man who developed programmed learning explain an associationist's views on the encouragement of inquiry and creativity; read some or all of these sections and record your reactions.

6–7   Sampling a Critical Appraisal of Learning by Discovery

One of the main arguments for discovery learning is that it helps pupils learn to solve problems *as* they learn about other things, whereas with programmed instruction it is necessary to teach subject matter and techniques of productive thinking separately. In a 1965 conference several outstanding psychologists made a critical appraisal of this and other claims for the discovery approach. The proceedings of the conference were reported in *Learning by Discovery* (1966) edited by Lee S. Shulman and Evan R. Keislar. This book contains articles by Jerome S. Bruner (Chapter VII) and Robert B. Davis (Chapter VIII), reporting on favorable experiences with the discovery approach, critiques by M. C. Wittrock and Lee J. Cronbach (Chapters IV and V), and some "Psychological Insights" (Chapters X and XI), in which Robert M. Gagné analyzes the discovery approach with reference to his conditions of learning and Jerome Kagan does the same with reference to his types of thinkers. For arguments supporting and rejecting the hypothesis that by the discovery method students can learn how to solve problems *while* they are learning subject matter, read one or more chapters in *Learning by Discovery,* and then record your reactions to the arguments presented on both sides.

6–8   Finding Out More about Heuristics

The teacher of mathematics or physical sciences is likely to find Gyorgy Polya's *How to Solve It* paperback (1954) especially interesting. The concise set of guidelines it offers might be used in encouraging students to learn to solve problems. Even if you will not be teaching math or science, you may find Polya's description of heuristics helpful and thought-provoking (and of assistance in solving Agatha Christie mysteries). As you peruse this book, note your reactions, and if possible indicate what possibilities you see for heuristics in your classes.

6–9   Analyzing Your Own Experiences with Habitual Set and Functional Fixedness

The impact of factors that may interfere with students' attempts at problem solving will become clear if you analyze your own experiences with habitual set and functional fixedness. Can you remember any situations (academic or otherwise) in which use of a habitual approach to things prevented you from solving a problem? Can you remember any in which use of objects or techniques only in a "typical" way kept you from finding an easy solution? If you do not think immediately of situations like these, can you remember a time when you couldn't quite grasp a point, or a key idea eluded you at the moment you wanted it (while taking an exam, for example) only to pop into your mind later (as you were leaving a building *after* taking an exam, perhaps)? Describe any such occasions, and comment on how you might assist your students to overcome similar blocks to problem solving.

6–10   Reading about the Early Lives of Creative People

In *Cradles of Eminence* (1962), Goertzel and Goertzel describe the background of four hundred eminent people who have lived in the twentieth century. While not all of these famous individuals were creative, many of them were, and an analysis of the forces which molded their personalities sheds light on the kinds of environmental experiences that seem to predispose a gifted person to develop his potential. The chapter headings summarize the main subjects discussed: 1, "Homes Which Respected Learning and Achievement"; 2, "Opinionative Parents"; 3, "Failure Prone Fathers" (half of the fathers of the four hundred were failure prone); 4, "Dominating Mothers"; 5, "Smothering Mothers" (smothering mothers produced dictators or poets— or both); 6, "Troubled Homes" (percentages from troubled homes: actors, 100%; authoritarian politicians, 95%; novelists and playwrights, 89%; composers and musicians, 86%; and military leaders, 86%); 9, "Early Agonies"; 10, "Dislike of School and Teachers." Some of these chapter headings may lure you to browse through *Cradles of Eminence*. Record your reactions and try to relate points noted in the book to techniques for encouraging creativity in your classes.

6–11   Examining Some of Torrance's Views on Creativity

E. Paul Torrance has probably done more and written more about developing creativity in children than any other psychologist. For ways to stimulate your students to be as creative as possible—or at least to avoid squelching their creativity—look through one or several of Torrance's books or articles. *A Source Book for Creative Thinking* (1962) edited by S. Parnes and G. Harding contains an article by Torrance (as well as contributions by others). *Guiding Creative Talent* (1962) and *Gifted Children in the Classroom* (1965) are more extensive discussions by Torrance. If you read any of these, note your reactions and comment on ideas you think might be worth trying with your students.

6–12   Reacting to "Teaching as a Subversive Activity"

Neil Postman and Charles Weingartner have written a book on American education with a provocative title. *Teaching as a Subversive Activity* (1969) diagnoses the ills of traditional education and proposes a panacea (a variation of the discovery approach). The authors present their case in lively if not vivid prose; the book reads as though it were dictated or written at a break-neck pace. While this makes for interesting reading, it has the disadvantage of rendering the discussion more than a little disorganized. Postman and Weingartner are convinced that the discovery approach as they practice it is *the* way to teach all subjects at all grade levels. Their faith in the absolute truth of their own convictions unfortunately leads them to reject and ridicule any other approach to teaching. For a sample of the style and tone of *Teaching as a Subversive Activity*—to see whether you care to read further—look at the list of proposals for improving education on pages 137–140. (Proposal 15 is: "Require that all the graffiti accumulated in the school toilets be reproduced on large paper and be hung in the school halls.") If you read this and other parts of the book, note points which you feel might be of value as you ponder ways to improve education.

Minimizing Forgetting, Maximizing Transfer

Key Points

Experiments

No increase in intelligence from study of any high school subject (Thorndike)

Concepts

Disuse, reorganization, repression, retroactive and proactive inhibition
Serial-position effect
Learning set
Positive transfer, negative transfer
"Real life" education

Principles

Positive relationship between transfer of principles and similarity of classroom situations to those pupils encounter outside
Necessity of teaching deliberately for transfer to insure transfer

Theories

Faculty psychology, doctrine of formal discipline

Methodology

Minimizing forgetting by overlearning, progressive part technique, emphasis on meaning and structure, recitation, and review
Making appropriate use of distributed practice, of whole and part procedures
Using Initial Teaching Alphabet (I.T.A.) approach in teaching reading
Teaching to encourage transfer

Chapter Contents

Testing and Organizing Your Knowledge of Key Points in Chapter 7

Experiments

At the beginning of this century there was a belief that the mind could be strengthened by exercise (based on the doctrine of formal discipline and on faculty psychology). It led to considerable emphasis on memorization and to arguments that "logical" subjects such as Latin and geometry would improve the mind. Edward L. Thorndike was in charge of a comprehensive study designed to test the hypothesis that such subjects might lead to overall gains in intelligence. In the spaces below describe the general conclusions of the Thorndike study and then comment on the impact they had on educational planning.

Conclusions of the Thorndike study

_____

_____

_____

_____

Impact these conclusions had on educational planning

_____

_____

_____

_____

Concepts

1. There are several explanations of why people forget. A knowledge of what is purported to cause forgetting may enable you to minimize such factors in your classroom. In the spaces below give a brief description and an example of each type of forgetting listed.

Disuse

_____

_____

_____

_____

_____

Reorganization

_____

_____

_____

_____

_____

Repression

_____

_____

_____

_____

_____

Interference

_____

_____

_____

_____

_____

2. When students are asked to learn lists of things, they may have difficulty because of the *serial position effect*. In the spaces below explain what this effect is, then describe how a teacher might minimize its impact.

Explanation of serial position effect

_____

_____

_____

_____

_____

How a teacher might minimize the impact of this effect

_____

_____

_____

_____

_____

3. Harry F. Harlow's experiments in which monkeys were presented with a series of related problems suggested to him that the animals developed a *learning set*. In many situations the development of learning sets is desirable, but sometimes it has undesirable consequences. In the spaces below explain what Harlow meant by a learning set, note how a learning set may cause difficulty, and tell how a teacher might counteract the negative influence of learning sets.

Explanation of a learning set

_____

_____

_____

_____

How a learning set may cause difficulty

_____

_____

_____

_____

How a teacher might counteract the negative influence of learning sets

_____

_____

_____

_____

_____

_____

4. One of the main goals of a teacher is to encourage transfer. Since transfer is so important, it is not surprising that there have been and continue to be differences of opinion about it. At one time it was believed that there might be transfer in terms of an increased intellectual capacity. The Thorndike study led to rejection of this hypothesis. Then it was thought that students should be given very specific training for "real life" experiences. Attempts to accomplish this goal have usually been ineffective. Becoming aware of *why* centering educational planning on "real" needs ordinarily fails might assist you to understand some of the difficulties in effecting transfer. In the space below comment on the possible limitations of concern for school experiences that are designed to be "relevant" only to current needs and situations. (Why might "education for relevance" be undesirable if it is stressed too much?)

_____

_____

_____

_____

_____

Principles

As opposed to trying to equip students with very specific training for certain situations and skills, a different approach appears to be more promising. A generally agreed upon interpretation of transfer was discussed in the opening chapter of the text, where the observations by Bruner were used to explain the rationale of this book, and in Chapter 6, where techniques for teaching problem solving were analyzed. In the following space outline two basic ideas now emphasized in encouraging transfer. (What types of learning might be stressed? How can a teacher increase the likelihood that what is learned will later be used?)

1. _____

_____

_____

_____

_____

_____

2. _____

_____

_____

_____

_____

_____

Methodology

1. The factors that cause forgetting (as you described them in item 1 under "Concepts") can be minimized by specific techniques. Listed below are several techniques for maximizing remembering. Explain and give an example of how you might use each one.

Overlearning

_____

_____

_____

_____

The progressive part technique

_____

_____

_____

_____

_____

Emphasis on meaning and structure

_____

_____

_____

_____

_____

Recitation

_____

_____

_____

_____

Review

_____

_____

_____

_____

2. Forgetting can also be minimized by the way you plan learning experiences in terms of time allowed and amount of material studied. In the spaces below describe learning situations in which you might use *distributed practice* periods, and the types of students and subject matter that might be approached through the *whole method*.

Use of distributed practice periods

_____

_____

_____

_____

Use of the whole method

_____
_____
_____
_____
_____
_____

3. If you take into account the points you mentioned on transfer in the preceding section ("Principles"), what two guidelines might you follow in teaching so as to encourage general transfer?

a. _____
_____
_____
_____

b. _____
_____
_____
_____

Suggestions for Further Reading, Thinking, and Discussion

7–1 Sampling Other Discussions of Forgetting and Transfer

The analysis of forgetting and transfer presented in Chapter 7 is brief and circumscribed. A different and perhaps more comprehensive overview of these two aspects of learning is available in other texts in educational psychology. If you would like more information, pick out two or three promising-looking recent publications at a library. You are sure to find at least a section if not a chapter devoted to forgetting and transfer. Read the appropriate sections of other texts, and outline points which impress you as informative or potentially valuable. If you would like to peruse a concise but complete analysis of transfer, look for *The Transfer of Learning* (1965) by Henry Ellis. Excellent observations on forgetting and transfer for the elementary teacher appear in Chapters 9 and 10 of *A Teacher's Guide to the Learning Process* (2nd ed., 1961) by May V. Seagoe.

7–2 Discovering English History as It Is Remembered

If you will be teaching history, or have ever taken a course in the history of England, try to find a copy of *1066 and All That* (1931; paperback ed., 1958) by Walter Carruthers Sellar and Robert Julian Yeatman. This is a description of English history as it might be recounted by a self-confident person who never learned it very well in the first place and who "reorganized" the few ideas which made an impression, filling in gaps as necessary. Chapter XLIX, for example, is devoted to "The Industrial Revelation" ("the discovery that women and children could work for 25 hours a day in factories without many of them dying or becoming excessively deformed"). In case you are unable to find this book, take a stab at writing your *own* version of a segment of history (or physics or chemistry or geography or whatever). Choose a subject you studied earlier in your academic career and compose a three- or four-page description of it. First note the few miscellaneous points you think you remember. Then let yourself go and fill in the gaps. (Write as if whatever you record will be taken as gospel by an audience of completely naive people who think you are the world's foremost authority.) After completing your account, read it and reflect on the recollection and transfer of information you once learned. If you don't remember much, does this mean you wasted your time when you studied the subject? Would you suggest dropping courses in that subject from the curriculum? If you hadn't taken that course, how would you have discovered whether it had or did not have meaning to you? Do you feel that a few miscellaneous recollections—even garbled ones—are better than no recollections at all?

7–3 Tuning in on the Thoughts of Children

Because they may not have matured intellectually to the point of understanding certain ideas, because ideas tend to become generalized, and because of the impact of forgetting, your students may have idiosyncratic notions about many things. You will discover this as soon as you start reading papers and exams, but meanwhile look for two assortments of gems of childish thought: *Write Me a Poem, Baby* (1956), and *Don't Get Perconel with a Chicken* (1959), both by H. Allen Smith. Art Linkletter has published similar collections of children's observations, but some of the reactions were obtained under rather contrived circumstances. Even so, you might enjoy browsing through *Kids Sure Rite Funny* (1962) or *A Child's Garden of Misinformation* (1965). As you sample any of these books, speculate on what you could do to prevent and/or correct for misconceptions and garbled recollections. If some of the statements reported by Smith or Linkletter appeared on your students' exams or papers, how would you react? For example, here is a composition (reproduced in *Don't Get Perconel with a Chicken*) entitled "Adults": "Adults dont do anything. Adults just sit and talk and dont do a thing. Theres not anything duller in this world than adultry." Would you simply enjoy them, or would you attempt to set their authors straight? How might you bring about discrimination if it is apparent that generalization has taken place? Are there any techniques for reducing children's tendency to draw false conclusions? Or is it preferable to attribute some interpretations to thought below the level of formal operations and simply let further maturation take care of things?

7–4 Learning English with H*Y*M*A*N K*A*P*L*A*N

Leo Rosten is an extremely versatile man who has been a reporter, Hollywood scriptwriter, author, and editor. When he was working on his Ph.D., he taught as a "bootleg substitute for an instructor in a night school." Out of his experiences came a novel about a teacher of special classes in English for immigrants who were applying for American citizenship. The book appeared under the pseudonym Leonard Q. Ross and was called *The Education of H*Y*M*A*N K*A*P*L*A*N* (1937). Hyman Kaplan was the "star" pupil in the class, and the way he came to grips with English illustrates all sorts of complications resulting from generalization, reorganized forgetting, and negative transfer. (For example, Mr. Kaplan refers to a newspaper as "he" rather than "it" because it is called the "Harold Tribune.") The further adventures of Mr. Kaplan—and of his teacher, Mr. Parkhill—are chronicled in *The Return of H*Y*M*A*N K*A*P*L*A*N* (1959). An English teacher will find these books especially enjoyable, but Hyman Kaplan has almost universal appeal. If you read either book, comment on the techniques Mr. Parkhill used in coping with Mr. Kaplan's interpretations of English. Then describe how you might have handled things if you had been the teacher.

7–5 Analyzing Your Thoughts about Team Teaching

Although team teaching is not practiced as widely as some of its early proponents expected it would be, many school systems do use this approach. You may find yourself faced with a choice between team teaching and a more self-contained approach when you consider job openings after earning your credential. To sort out your thoughts in regard to team teaching, look over *Team Teaching in Action* (1964) by Medill Bair and Richard G. Woodward, or a similar book on the subject, and compare the observations noted with those made by John A. Brownell and Harris A. Taylor in "Theoretical Perspectives for Teaching Teams," which appeared in Volume 43 (1962) of the *Phi Delta Kappan*. Or you might weigh different opinions by browsing through volumes of the *NEA Journal* or *The Instructor* (or the equivalent) for articles on this subject. Still another way to get information would be to interview one or more public school teachers who have participated in team teaching. Or list your own opinions regarding advantages and disadvantages. Regardless of how you approach the task, record your reactions for and against.

7–6   Analyzing Paleolithic Education

As a young instructor of future teachers Harold Benjamin was struck by what he considered absurdities in American education. He found release from his frustration with the "educational establishment" by writing a satire—*The Saber-Tooth Curriculum*—under the pseudonym J. Abner Peddiwell. In a series of imaginary "lectures," a professor of education describes how education was conducted in Paleolithic times. Even though *The Saber-Tooth Curriculum* was written in 1939, many of the sacred cows ridiculed by Benjamin thirty years ago are still with us. If you enjoy satire, this book will both entertain and enlighten you. If you read *The Saber-Tooth Curriculum,* relate Benjamin's criticisms of education to current trends and practices in the schools.

7–7   Taking a Closer Look at I.T.A.

The English language developed with no thought to the problems of generalization or negative transfer. The unsuspecting child is forced to deal with all kinds of inconsistencies. For example, a first-grader learns how to write *I* and then discovers that it is wrong to use *I* for *eye* or *aye*. Because English is not a phonetic language, the regular alphabet causes many problems for children learning to read. (There are twenty-two different ways the sound of *I* is spelled in different words.) Sir James Pitman's Initial Teaching Alphabet is an attempt to counteract some of the confusing elements of written English. If you will be teaching at the primary level, you might find it of interest to examine some I.T.A. materials in a curriculum library. Look through a series of books printed in I.T.A., paying attention to the way the transition is made from Pitman's special alphabet to the regular alphabet. Then note what you consider advantages of the I.T.A. as well as disadvantages. (For example, what sort of negative transfer might result from differences between the two alphabets?) If possible, interview a teacher who has used I.T.A. materials and ask for her reactions, positive and negative.

STUDY GUIDE

Teaching Skills and
Attitudes

	Key Points
Trends	Echoes of progressivism, which peaked in 1940's, in "learning for relevance"
Classifications	Taxonomy of educational objectives, affective domain (Krathwohl, Bloom, Masia)
Studies	Edge of progressivism over traditional education (Eight-Year Study) Insignificant impact of college education on student values (Jacob)
Concepts	Chaining Task analysis Beta hypothesis (Dunlap) Learning curve, plateau
Methodology	Making a task analysis and using chaining, demonstration, and guidance to help students master skills Taking learning curve into account to help students master skills and techniques Noting desirable attitudes and values and providing learning experiences to lead to their development

STUDY GUIDE

Chapter Contents

Testing and Organizing Your Knowledge of Key Points in Chapter 8

Classifications

As a teacher you will be concerned not only with cognitive objectives centering around the mastery of subject matter, but also with achieving certain *affective* objectives. Shifts in student attitudes are more likely if you try to move toward that goal systematically. In the spaces below describe the general nature and purposes of the *Taxonomy of Educational Objectives: Affective Domain* and explain how you might make use of this classification in planning instructional activities designed to develop particular attitudes and values.

Nature and purposes of the taxonomy of affective objectives

_____

_____

_____

_____

_____

How this taxonomy might be used

_____

_____

_____

_____

_____

Experiments

1. At the present time there is considerable agitation against a "strict," "traditional," "teacher-dominated" curriculum. In many respects current interest in a more "open-ended," "student-centered," "free" approach to education is similar to the enthusiasm for the progressive education of the 1930's and 1940's. For that reason the ambitious attempt to compare progressive and traditional education which was reported in *The Eight-Year Study* is significant. In the spaces below describe the experimental design of this investigation, summarize the major conclusions, and comment on why the study had relatively little impact on American education.

Experimental design of the Eight-Year Study

_____

_____

_____

_____

Major conclusions

_____

_____

_____

Why study had so little impact

_____

_____

_____

_____

2. One reason progressive education was shunted aside in the 1950's was the renewed concern for intellectual training. This was sparked by such diverse influences as awareness that the "whole child" approach had led to an erosion of academic standards, the fact that certain aspects of Russian technology had forged ahead of some aspects of American technology, and demands on the part of humanists (such as Arthur Bestor) that we return to emphasis on development of the intellect. Before progressivism became fashionable, it had been argued (and assumed) that a liberal, traditional education not only trained the mind, but inculcated desirable attitudes and values. The same argument was reintroduced by those who favored a return to classical education. Philip E. Jacob tested this hypothesis in a comprehensive study he reported in *Changing Values in College*. In the spaces below summarize Jacob's general conclusions and comment on how they might be used in planning instructional activities intended to foster the development of selected attitudes and values.

General conclusions of the Jacob study

_____

_____

_____

_____

_____

_____

_____

How these conclusions might be taken into account in planning instructional activities

_____

_____

_____

_____

_____

_____

_____

_____

_____

Concepts

1. One of Robert M. Gagné's conditions of learning is *chaining,* a concept which is often of value in planning skill-learning activities. In the space below explain and give an example of chaining.

_____

_____

_____

_____

_____

_____

2. The first step in any programmed learning approach is to describe the terminal behavior desired. When this is applied to skill learning, the description of terminal behavior takes the form of a *task analysis.* In the space below explain and give an example of a task analysis.

_____

_____

_____

_____

_____

_____

_____

3. Knight Dunlap proposed an explanation and suggested a remedy for certain bad habits. In the space below explain and give an example of how Dunlap's *Beta hypothesis* might be put into practice.

_____

_____

_____

_____

_____

4. When the development of a skill is plotted on a learning curve, a *plateau* often appears. In the space below explain, give an example of, and comment on the significance of a plateau.

_____

_____

_____

_____

_____

_____

_____

_____

Methodology

1. Depending on the subject you teach, you may spend some or most of your time assisting students to master skills of one kind or another. In the space below describe how you could encourage students to master a particular skill. If appropriate, explain how you might use task analysis and chaining, as well as *demonstration* and *guidance*.

_____

_____

_____

_____

_____

_____

_____

_____

2. It will be easier to foster and maintain interest in the learning of a skill if you take into account the shape of a typical learning curve. In the space

below describe how what has been discovered about learning curves (including plateaus) could help your students master skills.

_____

_____

_____

_____

_____

_____

3. Depending on the subject you teach, you may wish to encourage the development of certain attitudes and values. The first step will be to state your objectives in the affective domain as specifically as possible, perhaps with reference to the taxonomy you described earlier. What procedures follow? In the space below describe the fostering of a given attitude or value. (How would you proceed? What would you do?)

_____

_____

_____

_____

_____

_____

_____

_____

_____

Suggestions for Further Reading, Thinking, and Discussion

8–1   Playing the Role of an Efficiency Expert

When a teacher or psychologist performs a task analysis, he is functioning in the same way as an efficiency expert in a modern industrial concern. Time-and-motion studies are frequently carried out in industry and the military in order to find the most efficient way for workers or soldiers to do a given task and also to facilitate instruction. In certain business and military situations, where a devotee of task analysis is in charge, virtually *everything* is done "by the numbers." To become more aware of the pros and cons of making a task analysis and chaining the steps to be followed in acquiring a skill, imagine that you are a dedicated efficiency expert. Describe how routine activities (such as getting dressed or eating breakfast) could be made as efficient as possible, or how a task-analysis fanatic might set up a family schedule to increase efficiency around the house, or select some other activity of your own choosing. After you have written your satire, analyze it and note any points it illustrates about the pros and cons of performing a task analysis.

8–2 Checking on the Possibility of Analytic and "Global" Types

Jerome Kagan has described impulsive or reflective and analytic or thematic types of thinkers. It seems likely that there are also differences in the way individuals function physically. For example, some students respond more readily to a programmed approach to learning a skill; others prefer a discovery approach. Furthermore, certain skills ideally call for a step-by-step treatment, whereas in other types of performance individuality and freedom might be limited by a standard way of doing things. If you expect to be teaching a variety of skills, which ones might you subject to a programmed technique and which ones might be taught in a more open-ended fashion? How would you handle a "global" type of student who balked at step-by-step methods of instruction or an analytic type who seemed lost when told to "just go at it"? Would you insist that all students learn the same skill in the same way?

8–3 Analyzing Demonstrations You Have Witnessed

Demonstrations are a very common pedagogical device. If you would like to sort out your thoughts with regard to this form of teaching, think back to good and bad experiences you have had with teachers who used this method of instruction. Describe the best and the worst demonstrations you can remember. Then analyze why you were favorably or unfavorably impressed and try to compose a set of guidelines to follow when *you* give demonstrations.

8–4 Analyzing Experiences with Negative Transfer

The negative-transfer effect which a previously learned skill may have on the mastery of a new skill can be exasperating, time-consuming, and frustrating. Think back to skills you have learned and try to recollect any problems you encountered due to negative transfer. One student, for example, had learned to play the violin and then decided to take piano lessons. On his violin music, the numeral *1* appeared over the notes to be played with the first finger. On his piano music, the numeral *1* was placed over the notes to be played with the *thumb*. It was so difficult to overcome the tendency to use his first finger in response to a *1* in the music that the student gave up piano lessons in disgust. Analyze this situation, or a similar one you experienced yourself, and describe how you might assist someone to overcome the confusion induced by negative transfer. (If you had been the teacher of the piano student, how might you have helped him use the thumb rather than the first finger?)

8–5   Analyzing Experiences with a Plateau

Many learning curves have plateaus. You will surely recall learning situations in which you reached a point of no apparent improvement, only to go on eventually to a higher level of performance. Describe such an experience and then indicate what a teacher might have done to help you cope with or overcome the plateau in your curve of learning.

8–6   Designing a Curriculum to Accomplish the Goals
of the Eight-Year Study

The purpose of the Eight-Year Study was put in these terms:

> We are trying to develop students who regard education as an enduring quest for meaning rather than credit accumulation; who desire to investigate, to follow the leadings of a subject, to explore new fields of thought; knowing how to budget time, to read well, to use sources of knowledge effectively and who are experienced in fulfilling obligations which come with memberships in the school or college community. (Aikin, 1942, p. 144)

In many ways those words describe what contemporary college students often feel should be the purpose of higher education. Assume you are placed in charge of developing a new college. How will you organize the curriculum, plan classes, and carry out evaluation to achieve the purpose outlined above (or a credo you yourself evolved)? After describing your "ideal college," analyze it with reference to some realities of higher education in the United States today—a high student-teacher ratio, limited funds, the "demand" for some measure of academic achievement. Could changes be effected *within* the present structure of higher education to bring it closer to your "ideal"? Or would a complete departure be necessary?

8–7   Comparing Your Own Experiences with Those Reported
in the Jacob Study

The general conclusion of Philip E. Jacob's report on changing values in college was that teachers rarely had any effect on student attitudes. Analyze your own perception of the impact college has had on your attitudes and values and compare your analysis with Jacob's findings. Have any of your college teachers had a recognizable influence on your feelings about a particular subject or your general philosophy of life? Can you describe the qualities these teachers had? Were these qualities a function of a charismatic personality, or of the way the person conducted himself, or both? Would it be possible for anyone to achieve the same effect if he used the same approach?

8–8   Programming Attitudes in "Walden Two"

One of the most striking features of B. F. Skinner's Utopia described in *Walden Two* centers around the way desirable attitudes are reinforced and undesirable attitudes eliminated. The novel describes child-rearing techniques which encourage perseverance and patience and eliminate jealousy. If the possibility of shaping attitudes and values interests you, read Chapters 12, 13, and 14 of *Walden Two*. Record your reactions, first noting whether you think the techniques would *really* work if used exactly as described in the novel, then indicating whether you think similar techniques are applicable in a typical American home or classroom.

8–9   Using Programmed Techniques in Developing Vocational Instruction

Programmed instruction is rather common in military and industrial situations for teaching skills of various kinds. If you will be teaching a course which involves training in specific skills, you are urged to purchase a copy of *Developing Vocational Instruction* (1967) by Robert F. Mager and Kenneth M. Beach, Jr. The authors have had wide experience in industry, in behavioral research, and in teaching. In their words, *"Developing Vocational Instruction* is designed to aid both the skilled craftsman who is preparing instruction through which to teach his craft, and the experienced vocational or technical instructor who is interested in improving his present course or finds it necessary to prepare a new one." They also point out, however, that the book "is not specific to subject matter or vocation, and it applies to many academic as well as vocational and technical areas." If you will be teaching a craft or vocational skill, or if you would like to know how to make a job description, carry out a task analysis, derive course objectives, and develop lesson plans (among other things), read *Developing Vocational Instruction* and note your reactions.

Part Four / Motivation

Motivation:
Theory and Applications

Key Points

Classifications   Hierarchy of needs: physiological, safety, belongingness and love, esteem, self-actualization, knowing and understanding, aesthetic (Maslow)

Experiments   Setting of realistic goals by successful students, unrealistic goals by students who have failed (Sears)
Superiority of praise over blame as a motivating factor (Hurlock)
Incentive value of personal comments on papers (Page)

Concepts   Level of aspiration (Hoppe)
Positive aspects of competition; importance of standards (Gardner)
Desirability of a free, self-demand approach in students (Neil and Holt)

Theories   Behaviorism: deficit motivation
Psychoanalysis: striving for equilibrium
Equilibration (Piaget)
Growth motivation (Maslow)
Stimulation (White)

Methodology   Using behavior objectives, e.g., Goal Cards, to motivate (programmed approach)
Inducing dissatisfaction in the life space to motivate (discovery approach)
Using nondestructive competition to motivate
Encouraging the setting and maintaining of realistic levels of aspiration
Making the most of praise; reducing the negative impact of blame

Chapter Contents

Testing and Organizing Your Knowledge of Key Points in Chapter 9

Classifications

Abraham H. Maslow has classified human needs in terms of a hierarchy. This approach to analyzing motivation can help you understand why and how your students will react (or fail to react) to different situations. In the spaces below list the seven needs of Maslow's hierarchy in the proper sequence. Then comment on how this hierarchy can give you insight into the behavior of your students. (In your discussion, emphasize the difference between *deficiency* needs and *growth* needs.)

Maslow's hierarchy of needs

_____

_____

_____

_____

_____

How the hierarchy might be used in understanding student behavior

_____

_____

_____

_____

_____

_____

_____

_____

Experiments

1. Pauline Sears conducted an experiment to test the hypothesis of the German psychologist Hoppe that the behavior of students is influenced by their level of aspiration. In the spaces below describe the experimental design of the Sears study, then comment on how the results of this study might be used as the basis for helping students develop realistic levels of aspiration.

Experimental design of Sears study

_____

_____

_____

_____

Results of Sears study and implications of results for assisting students to develop realistic levels of aspiration

_____

_____

_____

_____

_____

_____

_____

2. A number of studies have analyzed the impact of praise and blame on student behavior. In the spaces below summarize some of their conclusions and comment on the implications of these conclusions.

Conclusions of studies on praise and blame

_____

_____

_____

_____

_____

_____

Implications of conclusions

_____

_____

_____

_____

_____

_____

Concepts

1. John Gardner's *Excellence* is a thoughtful analysis of the values and dangers of competition. At the present time many students are eager to sharply reduce or completely eliminate competition in school. In the space below comment on some of the unfortunate trends which Gardner suggests might emerge if competition were eliminated.

_____

_____

_____

_____

_____

2. A. S. Neill and John Holt hold to a conception of education which allows for maximum freedom. In a sense they believe in "self-demand" education. The text notes a number of possible limitations of this approach. In the spaces below explain what you regard as two of the major advantages and two of the major disadvantages of a Summerhill type of education.

Advantages

a. _____

_____

_____

b. _____

_____

_____

Disadvantages

a. _____

_____

_____

b. _____

_____

_____

_____

Theories

There are many theories regarding causes of behavior. Behaviorists stress one point of view, psychoanalysts another; Jean Piaget emphasizes *equilibration,* Abraham Maslow argues for *need gratification* (or growth motivation), Robert White stresses *stimulation theory.* In the spaces below give a brief description of each point of view.

Behaviorist's view of motivation

_____

_____

_____

_____

_____

Psychoanalyst's view of motivation

_____

_____

_____

_____

_____

Piaget's theory of equilibration

_____

_____

_____

_____

_____

Maslow's theory of need gratification

_____

_____

_____

_____

_____

_____

_____

White's stimulation theory

_____

_____

_____

_____

_____

Methodology

1. An associationist is likely to stress goals stated in behavioral terms as a means for assisting students to reach educational objectives. One specific device for doing this is a *Goal Card*. In the following space explain how a Goal

Card (or the equivalent) could motivate students in a manner consistent with the principles of programmed instruction.

_____

_____

_____

_____

_____

_____

2. A field theorist is likely to think in terms of the *life space* when he seeks to motivate students. One basic technique for making a student want to solve a problem is to induce a *sense of dissatisfaction* in his life space. In the space below explain and give an example of how you might motivate your students in a manner consistent with the principles of the discovery approach.

_____

_____

_____

_____

_____

_____

3. Competition has many unfortunate by-products. With care and ingenuity, however, you should be able to promote relatively nondestructive competition as you encourage students to work up to capacity. In the spaces below note two possible techniques for doing this.

a. _____

_____

_____

b. _____

_____

_____

4. The desirability of a realistic level of aspiration was demonstrated by Sears. In the space below note three general techniques for getting students to set realistic levels of aspiration.

a. _____

_____

_____

b. _____

_____

_____

c. _____

_____

_____

5. Certain forms of praise seem to be especially effective in motivating students to continue to do their best; certain types of blame or ridicule seem to have an opposite effect. In the spaces below describe how you might make the most of the positive impact of praise while reducing the negative impact of blame.

How you might try to make the most of praise

_____

_____

_____

_____

Techniques for reducing the negative impact of blame

_____

_____

_____

_____

_____

Suggestions for Further Reading,
Thinking, and Discussion

9–1   Reading Maslow's Own Account of His Theory of Need Gratification

The second edition of Abraham H. Maslow's *Toward a Psychology of Being* (1968) is filled with so much insight into so many aspects of human behavior and adjustment that you are urged to buy a copy for repeated reference. The headings of the major sections of the book indicate the general topics discussed: Part I, "A Larger Jurisdiction for Psychology"; Part II, "Growth and Motivation"; Part III, Growth and Cognition"; Part IV, "Creativeness"; Part V, "Values"; Part VI, "Future Tasks." If you have time only to sample the book at the moment, read Chapter 1, in which Maslow describes his conception of sickness and health; Chapter 3, in which he differentiates between deficiency and growth needs; Chapter 11, in which he contrasts bad choosers and good choosers; or Chapter 14, in which he lists forty-three basic propositions of a growth and self-actualization psychology. (The propositions in Chapter 14 pretty much summarize all his observations on motivation.) Summarize the points made in any parts of *Toward a Psychology of Being* you read, and add your own observations.

9–2   Reading a General Analysis of Motivation

The treatment of motivation in Chapter 9 is limited and oversimplified. For more background, read an appropriate chapter in a text in general psychology or introduction to psychology. If you still have the text you used in a psychology course, you might reread the discussion of motivation. Or select two or three promising introduction-to-psychology books at the library. If you find a concise analysis of motivation, summarize it and relate it to points made in the text.

9–3   Analyzing Your Own Motivation

Insight into theories of motivation sometimes results from self-analysis. How energetically do you pursue different goals? Do you have a fairly consistent level of aspiration, or do you exert yourself in only a few areas of behavior? What forces drive you to try to achieve at a high level in certain activities? Can you relate your drives to psychological needs? Do you sometimes feel compelled to regain a sense of equilibrium? Do you engage in some of your activities as a means to "expression"? If those questions do not seem simple to answer, analyze your behavior at different times in terms of Maslow's hierarchy. Do you find evidence that you are more likely to want to learn or to satisfy an aesthetic desire when your lower-level needs have been taken care of? If you note exceptions, how might you explain them? (E.g., are thoughts of hunger and discomfort displaced by the sight of the love of your life?) If you gain any insight into your own motives, describe and comment on your self-analysis.

9–4   Analyzing the Forces Which Shaped Famous People

In speculations about what motivates people to strive and achieve, the question of determinism is of key importance. Chapter 2 offered various observations on determinism, with special reference to two explanations of what factors "produced" Shakespeare. Was he primarily the product of contingencies of reinforcement, or did he inherit some sort of "divine spark" of inspiration? Now that you have more information on motivation, choose some famous person you know something about, or would like to learn about, and analyze —as best you can—the forces that made him great. Or browse through *Cradles of Eminence* (1962) by Goertzel and Goertzel and consider the common factors they found in the backgrounds of famous people. Is there evidence to back up Freud's suggestion that in some cases extreme efforts in the arts or politics are due to sublimation of the sex drive? Or analyze the lives of the eminent people described by Goertzel and Goertzel (or any group of your own choice) with reference to Shakespeare's "theory" of motivation: "Some are born great, some achieve greatness, and some have greatness thrust upon them." You may conclude that psychologists haven't come up with any better way to summarize motivation since those words were written over 350 years ago. If any of these questions or suggestions appeal to you, record your reactions.

9–5   Analyzing the Forces Which Shaped Acquaintances

If you find it difficult to analyze your own behavior and feel more attuned to the present than the past, you might turn your attention to the forces that influenced individuals you have known. Can you think of an acquaintance who appears to have a tremendous desire to succeed in certain areas of endeavor? What forces in his background might have made him that way? After you record your speculations, try to relate them to one or more of the theories of motivation which have been discussed and comment on any implications that seem to emerge.

9–6   Contrasting Bad- and Good-Choice Situations

Maslow makes a distinction between bad and good choosers. To become more aware of what he means by this, analyze your own feelings and behavior with regard to choice situations. Maslow describes growth as a never-ending series of decisions between safety and growth and suggests that a person is more likely to make a good choice if he feels confident and self-accepting. If the person feels threatened, he may be unable to resist selecting a safe—but perhaps undesirable—form of behavior. Think back to choice situations you have faced recently. When you decided to try something and it proved to be an exhilarating experience, did you feel confident and self-accepting prior to the decision? Can you figure out what made you that way? If you procrastinated about a choice and finally took a safe way out by avoiding the situation or reacting in a manner that provided little if any satisfaction, what was it that made you feel threatened? Could you—or someone else—have reduced the threat somehow? If possible, relate your analysis to how you might function as a teacher. What could you do to establish a classroom environment where your students would feel confident and unthreatened enough to make good choices and have more frequent self-actualizing experiences?

9–7   Analyzing Level of Aspiration

Maslow's distinction between bad and good choosers is essentially a generalized version of Hoppe's observations on the level of aspiration. Hoppe suggested that a person's level of aspiration in a given situation is a compromise between two conflicting tendencies: (1) the desire to avoid disappointment accompanying failure, which operates to force aspirations down, and (2) the desire to succeed at the highest possible level, which pushes aspirations up. If you find it difficult to analyze a choice between safety and growth as suggested in exercise 9–6, you might attempt an analysis of your level of aspiration in one or two situations. For example, at the beginning of a course when you determined the grade level you hoped to achieve, what factors influenced your decision? If the evaluation in the course seemed to be threatening, did you set your aspirations at the "C" level? How did you react when you got your grade on the first exam? If you set your aspiration level low for one course and high for another, what factors influenced your decision? Record your reactions to one or more of these questions and then describe how you might assist *your* students to set high—but realistic—levels of aspiration. What could you do to help them achieve a desirable compromise between the two tendencies to avoid disappointment and to succeed at the highest possible level?

9–8   Speculating about the Pros and Cons of a Structured Curriculum

A. S. Neill argues that a free, self-demand approach to education is most likely to permit a child to respond favorably to learning experiences. He is against any sort of structured curriculum, particularly one in which a student is required to take certain courses or to learn material predetermined by a teacher. Robert Gagné, on the other hand, believes that students learn best when learning experiences are arranged systematically so that verbal associations serve as the basis for concepts and principles, which eventually lead to problem solving. Inevitably, this approach involves direction by a teacher who "requires" students to learn certain things in a certain way. If you are undecided about these two points of view, think about the subject or subjects you will be teaching. Could some topics be approached in a free way whereas others might need to be prearranged and presented in sequence? A different way of looking at this question would be to think about courses you have taken. Would you have preferred more freedom with some subjects, and did you wish the instructor had been better organized and done more structuring with others? Note your reactions to either of these sets of ideas, and comment on the implications.

9–9   Analyzing the Advantages and Disadvantages of Competition

At the present time in American education there is a move to reduce competition between students. Excessive competition obviously has many disadvantages, most disturbingly the amount of threat involved, which tends to lead to safety rather than growth choices. But competition has values too, and certain dangers would follow if all competitive effort were eliminated. John Gardner, former Secretary of Health, Education and Welfare, has analyzed the problem of encouraging and maintaining constructive striving in the United States in three short books. *Excellence* (1961) stresses the importance of high standards. *Self-Renewal* (1965) examines ways individuals and societies might resist the negative impact of apathy and lowered motivation. *No Easy Victories* (1968) describes the difficulties of achieving and maintaining excellence and self-renewal. If you have the opportunity to read one of these books (all three are quite concise), summarize Gardner's views and state your reactions.

9–10   Assessing Your Reactions to the Committee Approach

You may find it helpful to assess any personal experiences you have had with the committee approach in order to decide whether, when, and how to use this technique when you teach. If you have been a member of a committee, record your reactions, perhaps by listing desirable and undesirable aspects of the experience. Then describe how you might make the most of the things you liked while eliminating or reducing the disadvantages. If you feel enthusiastic about group learning, sample Chapters 7, 8, and 9 of *Education and the Human Quest* (1960) or Chapters 1, 2, and 10 of *Classroom Grouping for*

Teachability (1967), both by Herbert A. Thelen. Thelen, probably the leading exponent of the group approach, has much to offer. In case you read sections of either of these books, summarize the points made by Thelen and add your own reactions.

9–11   Recording Your Own Reactions to Praise and Blame

You may be more alert to the impact of praise and blame on student behavior if you record your own reactions to these two types of teacher response. Think back to teachers you had, and to specific incidents in which you (or a classmate) were exposed to desirable kinds of praise or undesirable kinds of blame. When you were praised for doing well, what were your reactions? If you were ridiculed or humiliated or severely criticized for poor schoolwork (not for deportment), what were your reactions? Can you recall any experiences which were so distasteful you still have a negative emotional response just thinking about them? After recording your recollections, comment on the implications and perhaps draw up a list of do's and don'ts to follow when *you* become the person who dispenses praise or blame.

9–12   Reacting to a Humorous Programmer's Views on Goals and Motivation

Robert F. Mager (coauthor of *Developing Vocational Instruction,* which was recommended to you for reading in one of the exercises suggested for Chapter 8) is an advocate of programmed instruction. Most psychologists who are attracted by the more precise and technological aspects of teaching seem to suppress any hint of levity in their writing. Mager, however, has an irrepressible sense of humor. His two short books mix humor and common sense with practical suggestions on how to use programmed instruction in motivating students. Both books are available in paperback and would be valuable additions to any teacher's professional library. In *Preparing Instructional Objectives* (1962), Mager suggests how educational objectives can be specified in such a way that students are encouraged to demonstrate their achievement of the objectives. In *Developing Attitude Toward Learning* (1968), he offers observations on how to teach so that your pupils will have more favorable feelings about your subject after studying under your direction than before they met you. (From one point of view, this is the single most important goal a teacher should try to reach.) If you read either or both of these books, note points made by Mager which strike you as especially promising and indicate how you might use these ideas when you begin to teach.

10

Teaching
the Disadvantaged

Key Points

Facts

Problems of the disadvantaged: diet, health, moves, test-taking difficulties, poor language skills, preference for physical learning, slow learning rate

Trends

Growth of Head Start from brief summer project to program lasting several years

Reports

Benefits of compensatory education (Deutsch)

Many causes of the disadvantaged's difficulty in responding to learning experiences; correspondence of rioters and dropouts (Riot Commission Report)

Deterrent effect on learning of grouping disadvantaged children with other slow learners (Coleman Report)

Concepts

Destiny control (Coleman)

Methodology

Taking into account the lack of motivation of disadvantaged children
Considering the history, culture, and background of minority-group students
Taking into account the learning problems of disadvantaged pupils

Chapter Contents

Testing and Organizing Your Knowledge of Key Points in Chapter 10

Facts

Reports on students with disadvantaged backgrounds have been consistent in emphasizing certain factors. Listed below are several well-established facts which summarize these findings. For each point noted, comment on how a teacher might ameliorate, compensate for, or take into account the characteristic or condition described.

Disadvantaged children are likely to have a poor diet and suffer from health problems.

_____

_____

_____

_____

Students of disadvantaged backgrounds are likely to move frequently.

_____

_____

_____

_____

_____

Lower-class children have difficulty taking tests.

_____

_____

_____

_____

_____

Disadvantaged children tend to be relatively poor in language skills.

_____

_____

_____

_____

_____

Students from deprived homes usually favor physical over mental learning.

_____

_____

_____

_____

_____

Students from deprived homes tend to learn at a slower rate than those from nondeprived homes.

_____

_____

_____

_____

_____

Trends

The original Head Start programs were developed in accordance with the critical-period concept. Extra stimulation during the preschool years was supposed to give the child sufficient background to cope with later schooling. It is now clear that a very common "fade" reaction occurs when Head Start experiences are terminated at the preschool level. Consequently, a new trend in the philosophy behind compensatory education has emerged. In the spaces below describe the nature of this trend and comment on its significance for teachers who will have disadvantaged students in their classes.

Emerging trend in philosophy of compensatory education

_____

_____

_____

_____

_____

Significance of trend for teachers

_____

_____

_____

_____

_____

Concepts

Equality of Educational Opportunity (the Coleman Report) places great emphasis on *destiny control*. In the spaces below describe what is meant by destiny control, and comment on the possible negative impact of ability grouping on disadvantaged students.

Description of destiny control

_____

_____

_____

_____

Possible impact of ability grouping on disadvantaged students

_____

_____

_____

_____

_____

Methodology

The *Report of the National Advisory Commission on Civil Disorders* stressed the need for teacher candidates to become familiar with the "psychology, history, culture and learning problems of minority group pupils." In Chapter 10 information intended to make you familiar with such factors formed the basis for suggestions on how to teach the disadvantaged.

In the space below note three techniques you might use to compensate for problems of poor motivation common to disadvantaged students.

1. _____

_____

_____

2. _____

_____

_____

3. _____

_____

_____

In the space below describe three ways to take into account and allow for the history, culture, and background of minority-group students.

1. _____

_____

_____

2. _____

_____

_____

3. _____

_____

_____

In the space below list three specific teaching techniques for counteracting learning problems common to disadvantaged students.

1. _____

_____

_____

2. _____

_____

_____

3. _____

_____

_____

Suggestions for Further Reading, Thinking, and Discussion

10–1   Sampling Sections of the Riot Commission Report

The *Report of the National Advisory Commission on Civil Disorders* is an exhaustive analysis of the causes of ferment in American society. It is organized around three questions: What happened? Why did it happen? What can be done? As a future teacher, you will probably find many sections of the Riot Commission Report interesting. Since the complete document is over seven hundred pages long, you may wish to read only sections of it. In that case, peruse Chapter 8, "Conditions of Life in the Racial Ghetto," or the section on education in Chapter 17, "Recommendations for National Action." If you read either of these sections, or others of your own choice, summarize the points made and add comments of your own.

10–2   Sampling Sections of "Equality of Educational Opportunity"

The Riot Commission Report presents a general analysis of the education of the disadvantaged. A more specific evaluation of problems of inequalities in education is offered in *Equality of Educational Opportunity* (the Coleman Report). The report itself is extremely detailed and lengthy, but you will find a brief analysis of the major conclusions drawn by Coleman, together with a review of criticisms made by others, in an article by Christopher Jencks,

"A Reappraisal of the Most Controversial Educational Document of Our Time," which appeared in the *New York Times Magazine* of August 10, 1969, or in an article by Catherine Caldwell titled "Social Science as Ammunition," which appeared in the September, 1970, issue of *Psychology Today.* If you read either of these articles or some other discussion of the Coleman Report, summarize the main points and note your own reactions.

10–3   Reading a Personal Account of Life in Ghetto Schools

The two formal reports noted in exercises 10–1 and 10–2 cover the educational problems of disadvantaged children in a comprehensive way. Within the last few years, several accounts of the experiences of individual teachers in ghetto schools have been published. Edward R. Braithwaite described what it was like to teach in a London slum in *To Sir, with Love* (1959). Bel Kaufman's *Up the Down Staircase* (1964), a fictional narration of life in a New York City high school, is probably the most widely read exposition of life in a big-city school. At about the time *Up the Down Staircase* was establishing itself on the best-seller lists, three young men were either starting or finishing descriptions of their experiences in ghetto schools. Jonathan Kozol accepted a position as a substitute teacher in a Boston elementary school. He held the position for about six months before he was dismissed, at which time he expanded the notes he had taken into *Death at an Early Age* (1967). Herbert Kohl told what it was like to be a teacher in a Harlem sixth grade in *36 Children* (1967), and James Herndon commented on academic life in an Oakland junior high school in *The Way It Spozed to Be* (1968). To sample a personal account of teaching in a ghetto school and how different individuals attempted to assist disadvantaged students to learn, look for one of these books. *36 Children* is especially recommended if you will be teaching at the elementary level; *Up the Down Staircase* if you will be teaching at the secondary level. Record your reactions, emphasizing techniques described in the book which you think you might try in your classes.

10–4   Sampling an Analysis of Teaching Techniques for the Disadvantaged

If you think you will eventually seek a position in a school with a high percentage of disadvantaged students, you might find it helpful to compile ahead of time a list of specific techniques for working with such pupils. Concisely described methods are to be found in an article by Patric Groff, "Culturally Deprived Children: Opinions of Teachers and Views of Riessman," in the October, 1964, issue of *Exceptional Children.* For more complete analyses you might peruse *The Disadvantaged Child: Issues and Innovations* (2nd ed., 1970) edited by Joe L. Frost and Glenn R. Hawkes, *The Disadvantaged*

Learner (1966) edited by Staten W. Webster, *Education in Depressed Areas* (1962) edited by Harry A. Passow, or *How to Teach Disadvantaged Youth* (1969) by Allen C. Ornstein and Philip D. Vairo, or a similar book you find in a library. Pick out the techniques which impress you as promising and compose a personal handbook of methods you could use for teaching the disadvantaged.

10–5   Sorting Out Your Thoughts on Ability Grouping

The Coleman Report suggested that placing disadvantaged children in the same class might produce a form of reciprocal fatalism. At present there is considerable controversy over desegregation in American schools. Attempts to integrate students of disadvantaged backgrounds into middle-class schools are often blocked or sidestepped in one way or another. Some educators argue that it is desirable to group students on the basis of ability. Advocates of this position might not be upset by segregation because such a policy leads to a form of ability grouping. Other educators, impressed by the Coleman Report, feel that any educational arrangement which separates students from rich and poor environments is undesirable since it perpetuates the tendency for the fortunate child to be given extra opportunities and for the unfortunate child to remain at a disadvantage. Those who favor ability grouping point out that merely placing a disadvantaged child in a room with middle-class pupils is not always beneficial; the student from a poor environment may be intimidated or humiliated by the ease and speed of learning demonstrated by his luckier classmates.

How the educational handicaps of the disadvantaged can be overcome is perhaps the most important problem of contemporary American education. Examine the issues and try to come up with your own solution. Perhaps you could describe an overall policy you would recommend and then list some specific interim measures to be used until a general solution is found.

10–6   Recording Your Reactions to Integrated Education

Attempts to "integrate" higher education are being made on many college campuses. Programs and scholarships provide minority-group students with increased opportunities to get a college education since a college degree is recognized as being almost a necessity for many types of jobs. When these programs were in the planning stage, it was hoped that interaction between students from different backgrounds would lead to the lowering of barriers between ethnic groups. This hope has seldom been realized because the members of some minority groups have tended to keep to themselves. In the very process of seeking identity, they have caused a polarizing rather than integrative reaction. If you have had any personal experience with such a situation, record your reactions. Can you think of any techniques or approaches which might permit minority-group students to maintain a sense of identity but also become "integrated" at the same time? In the absence of some form of interaction, how will minority groups ever become participating members of society at large? What are the advantages and disadvantages of reducing distinctions between different groups of Americans? If you have not been directly involved with this situation, but find the question to be of interest, you might read "The Road to the Top Is Through Higher Education—Not Black Studies" by Arthur Lewis, in the May 11, 1969, issue of the *New York Times Magazine*. Summarize the points made by Lewis and note your reactions.

10–7   Speculating about the Impact of "Skillful" Child Rearing

As reports of the "fade" reaction of Head Start programs have accumulated, some theorists have concluded that the failure of preschool experiences to have a permanent impact is due to too little, too late. It has been suggested that an intensive program of stimulation should start in infancy. Another proposal is that the child-rearing practices of different mothers should be observed, the performance of their children should be noted, and the techniques used by mothers who "produced" bright children should then be practiced by *all* mothers. Advocates of this approach predict that it will, in effect, lead to the development of uniformly bright children. Record your reactions. Do you favor the idea? Do you think it will work? Do you see any possible dangers or disadvantages? If you should read an analysis of the child-rearing techniques used by the parents of some highly successful person, would you feel confident about using the same techniques with your children?

10–8   Tuning in on "Sesame Street"

A different way to encourage children to make the most of their potential is made possible through the television series "Sesame Street." Watch one or more segments of this program, and compare an approach which allows a child to respond to ideas more or less on his own (by watching TV) to one in which parents "arrange" the environment for the child. What techniques used by "Sesame Street" might be used in your classes? (You will find that many of them can be related to points discussed in this book. For example, compare the descriptions of intellectual development proposed by Piaget and Bruner to the presentations on the program. Or look for the techniques of programmed instruction.)

Part Five / Evaluation

Evaluating Classroom Learning

Key Points

Classifications   Taxonomy of educational objectives

Criteria   Test evaluation criteria: standard situation, permanent record of behavior, and comparison with standard answers; validity and reliability

Experiments   Cheating by all children when stakes sufficiently high (Hartshorne and May)

Concepts   Halo effect, cognitive dissonance, projection, unconscious likes and dislikes
Importance of an adequate sample
Learning for mastery

Methodology   Writing and scoring classroom exams
Evaluating exams by item analysis
Assigning final grades
Drawing and interpreting frequency distributions
Computing and interpreting mean and median

Chapter Contents

Testing and Organizing Your Knowledge of Key Points in Chapter 11

Classifications

The taxonomy of educational objectives was first called to your ·attention with reference to learning and motivation. Lesson plans organized to make the most of structure will assist students to learn; a series of goals stated in behavioral terms will improve the *desire* of students to learn. Some sort of classification scheme will also be extremely helpful when the time comes to evaluate how much and how well your students have learned. In the space below explain how a classification scheme (such as the taxonomy of educational objectives) could make your evaluations systematic and effective. (Why should you be concerned about getting a good sample and how can you carry out this objective?)

_____

_____

_____

_____

_____

Criteria

1. When one person reacts to the behavior of another, it is difficult to control the influence of subjective factors. Formal tests are frequently used to minimize the impact of subjectivity. Typically, such measuring devices have three characteristics designed to help a teacher make objective evaluations. In the space below note these characteristics and explain how you might use each as a criterion for determining whether a given test is likely to reduce the effect of subjectivity. (Ask yourself, e.g., Does this test . . . ?)

a. _____

_____

_____

b. _____

_____

_____

c. _____

_____

_____

2. Those who specialize in evaluation usually assess a test with reference to two factors: *validity* and *reliability*. In the spaces below note the kinds of questions you would keep in mind as criteria for judging the validity and reliability of a test.

Validity

_____

_____

_____

Reliability

_____

_____

_____

Experiments

Hartshorne and May conducted an elaborate investigation of honesty. The results of this study might assist you to understand and reduce student cheating. In the spaces below summarize the general conclusions of the study and comment on their implications as far as minimizing cheating is concerned.

Conclusions of Hartshorne and May study

_____

_____

_____

_____

Implications for minimizing cheating

_____

_____

_____

_____

Concepts

1. Several psychological mechanisms relating to how the perceptions of individuals are influenced by subjective factors have been identified and described. Four of these concepts are listed below. Write an explanation and an example of how a teacher's perception of student behavior might be distorted by each mechanism.

Halo effect

_____

_____

_____

Cognitive dissonance

_____

_____

_____

Projection

_____

_____

_____

_____

_____

Unconscious likes and dislikes

_____

_____

_____

_____

_____

2. A new conception of evaluation is currently being offered as a means for reducing the negative impact of the traditional competitive approach to grading. In the spaces below give the rationale of *learning for mastery* and describe how such an approach might be put into practice.

Rationale of learning-for-mastery approach

_____

_____

_____

_____

_____

How it might be put into practice

_____

_____

_____

_____

_____

Methodology

1. It is almost inevitable that you will have to use tests of one kind or another. Consequently, you would do well to think ahead about writing and scoring tests. In the space below note three general guidelines or steps you might follow in writing and scoring tests.

a. _____

_____

b. _____

_____

c. _____

_____

2. As soon as you begin giving exams of your own, you will discover that a first attempt at writing an exam is rarely completely successful. Some questions are better than others, and some exams are better than others. To improve your tests—and also your teaching—it will be desirable to appraise your attempts at evaluation. A basic technique for doing this involves analyzing specific questions. In the space below describe how to perform an item analysis of an examination.

_____

_____

_____

_____

_____

3. Since you will almost certainly have to record your impressions of the academic (and perhaps social) performance of your pupils on report cards, it will be to your advantage to plan this procedure ahead. In the spaces below note three general guidelines for assigning final grades on report cards.

a. _____

_____

b. _____

_____

c. _____

_____

4. In order to analyze and compare the scores of different students, you will find it virtually a necessity to draw a frequency distribution for exams or total scores. Listed below are some hypothetical scores earned by twenty-five students on an exam. Prepare a frequency distribution for these scores. (After drawing your distribution, compare it with that depicted on page 235 of this Study Guide.)

40	41	30	44	42
38	39	37	39	39
29	38	46	32	40
47	35	45	43	34
32	33	37	40	38

5. Just looking at a frequency distribution gives some insight into the relative position of a student. But for a more systematic comparison of students you should calculate a measure of central tendency. In the spaces below note the *mean* and *median* of the distribution you drew for item 4 and explain how you arrived at each figure. (What procedure did you follow?) (After calculating the mean and median, check your answers with those provided on page 235 of this Study Guide.)

Mean of distribution drawn for item 4

_____

_____

_____

_____

_____

_____

Median of distribution drawn for item 4

_____

_____

_____

_____

_____

_____

6. While you and your students will want information about relative performance on specific exams, you will probably make greatest use of distributions and measures of central tendency when you assign final grades; assigning letter-grades on individual exams is difficult because of the homogeneity of scores. For insight into this problem, assume you are teaching an unselected (ungrouped) class and indicate the letter-grades you would assign on the distribution you drew for item 4. Are there truly clear-cut differences?

You may appreciate the desirability of obtaining a variety of measures of student performance if you examine the hypothetical page from a teacher's grade book depicted on the following page.

	First Exam (100 pts.)	Second Exam (100 pts.)	Third Exam (100 pts.)	First Project (50 pts.)	Second Project (50 pts.)	Totals
Adams, A.	78	83	81	41	39	322
Baker, C.	87	82	88	44	45	346
Cook, D.	68	72	71	30	32	273
Davis, R.	96	89	93	47	46	371
Evans, G.	73	77	75	39	42	306
Ford, H.	77	78	74	41	39	309
Gary, N.	81	79	82	72	42	356
Hood, B.	83	85	85	43	44	340
Ingram, R.	79	76	75	39	39	308
Jones, C.	67	63	66	31	32	259
Kent, P.	96	97	95	49	49	386
Landis, H.	90	89	92	47	46	364
Moore, J.	77	73	78	39	44	311
Norton, C.	75	83	86	39	47	330
Parker, N.	84	87	89	40	46	346
Quist, A.	88	86	84	46	45	349
Radke, L.	91	92	93	46	46	368
Smith, J.	56	54	52	27	23	212
Terry, R.	75	75	76	38	39	303
Unger, V.	78	74	73	41	40	306
Vance, A.	91	86	89	43	45	354
Ward, M.	81	84	87	44	44	340
York, C.	70	71	69	33	35	278
Zucker, A.	77	78	73	41	37	306

Suppose that this is an unselected class and that school guidelines suggest "A" for superior work, "B" for above average, "C" for average, "D" for just passing, and "F" for unsatisfactory work. Make a frequency distribution of the total scores (use a separate sheet of long, lined paper—or a lined piece of paper torn in half and taped to form a double-length sheet), calculate the median, and use it to determine who will get a "C." Then assign letter-grades for the other levels. It may be of interest to compare your work with a classmate's.

Suggestions for Further Reading, Thinking, and Discussion

11–1   Examining Your Own Dissatisfactions with Tests and Grades

Chapter 11 begins with a survey of student criticisms of tests and grades. If you have strong negative feelings about these matters too, draw up your own list of complaints, then analyze it to see whether the disagreeable aspects could be minimized or eliminated. As you describe your plan for reform, however, keep in mind conditions under which you are almost sure to have to work. For example, most teachers in American public schools are required to assign grades on an "A" to "F" scale (or the equivalent); the GPA of a student may determine his eligibility for college or for a job; parents will be just as interested in grades as their children (if not more interested). These points are mentioned so that you will think about ways to improve evaluation *within* the present structure of the public education system rather than proposing sweeping changes which would have little or no chance of being adopted in the schools.

11–2   Reacting to Arguments in Favor of Tests and Grades

A number of arguments in *favor* of tests and grades are noted in Chapter 11. Since you will soon be dispensing rather than receiving grades, try to be open-minded about these points. Does John Gardner's suggestion that grades motivate students to work up to high standards seem valid? According to Gardner, the schools are the primary agency for doing the preliminary sorting out of able and less able individuals in our society—in which performance is a major determinant of status. Do you feel that the schools should undertake this sorting? If you would prefer an approach to education in which comparisons between students were minimized, what alternative methods of selecting capable individuals can you propose? If GPA in high school is not used in determining who will be admitted to college, how *should* the limited number of openings in colleges be filled? Does competition for grades assist students to make the most of their abilities? By establishing and maintaining high standards, does a teacher help students set respectable levels of performance and gain experience that will permit rigorous self-analysis? Although you may feel bitter about grades, perhaps you should at least entertain the possibility that evaluation has some desirable aspects which ought to be retained even as we seek improvements in the overall system of evaluation currently in force in the schools. If this basic question interests you, record your thoughts on the subject in writing.

11–3   Speculating about Cheating

Whether or not you approve, the fact remains that the schools *do* perform the preliminary sorting out of able and less able individuals. You may question the kind of ability which current school practices "reward," but the GPA (or equivalent) is unlikely to diminish in importance within the next few years. Because considerable pressure to get high grades is exerted on students in American schools, a significant number of pupils feels driven to cheat. Analyze your own experiences and feelings regarding cheating as a first step to speculating about how pressure for grades could be reduced in your classes.

Knowing that you will almost surely be required to assign grades—probably with reference to some sort of distribution—what might you do to lessen your students' tendency to cheat? (As you record your thoughts, concentrate on specific techniques that might be applied within the present system.)

11–4   Analyzing Your Own Experiences with Subjectivity

To gain greater insight into the impact of mechanisms which interfere with objectivity, examine your own experiences with reference to the concepts noted in the text. Have you ever realized at a later time that your initial feelings about a certain individual were dominated by one good or bad characteristic which caused a halo effect? Did you ever find it difficult to believe an action or a report which was contrary to what you expected of an acquaintance? Could your irritation at a habit in someone else perhaps be due to your dislike of acknowledging that you have the same habit yourself? Have you ever reacted very favorably or unfavorably to an individual you met for the first time without understanding exactly why? Record one or more incidents of the type just described that you can recall, and draw any possible implications from them as you approach the point of interacting with large numbers of students.

11–5   Analyzing Tests with Reference to the Criteria Noted in the Text

You might be able to increase the likelihood that your first exams will bring about a favorable reaction in your students if you take the time to analyze exams *you* have especially liked and disliked. Write a description of the one you liked best and the one you liked least. Then refer to the characteristics of tests noted in Chapter 11. Did you favor a test which involved a permanent record of behavior that you and the teacher could reexamine as often as desired? Were your answers evaluated according to a reasonable, clear set of scoring standards? If the test you liked best did not have these characteristics, what *were* the qualities that made you respond favorably? If the test you disliked had some of these characteristics but still seemed unsatisfactory, why were you bothered? Record your reactions and, if possible, come up with a set of dos and don'ts to follow when you begin to make up exams.

11–6   Comparing Your Reactions to Objective and Essay Tests

The text makes a comparison between objective tests and essay exams. If you will be teaching at the secondary level, it might be of interest to carry out a similar analysis of your own. For example, you might compare observations made by Banesh Hoffmann in his book *The Tyranny of Testing* (1962) with those offered by Henry Chauncey and John E. Dobbin in *Testing: Its Place in Education Today* (1963). Hoffmann is a distinguished mathematician who felt that psychologists and educators were too involved in testing to recognize certain weaknesses and inconsistencies of objective tests. Chauncey is president of Educational Testing Service and Dobbin an influential member of the same company (the leading publisher of standardized tests). In Chapter 3 of *The Tyranny of Testing,* Hoffmann describes some problems of grading essay exams. In Chapter 4 he discusses "Objectivity and Ambiguity." Among other things he points out that *objective* is a misnomer, since the term refers only to the process of grading. The person who decides which multiple-choice answer is correct is making just as subjective a judgment as the person evaluating an essay answer. In Chapter 5 he criticizes the emphasis on the "best" answer and suggests that the person taking the test is required to attempt to fathom how the mind of the test-writer functions. In Chapter 6 he argues that multiple-choice tests discriminate against the brightest, most creative students. Chauncey and Dobbin present counterarguments in a section beginning on page 77 of *Testing: Its Place in Education Today* and in the Appendix: "Multiple-Choice Questions: A Close Look." If you are undecided about the relative merits, strengths, and weaknesses of multiple-choice and essay tests, compare the views of Hoffmann with those of Chauncey and Dobbin, or make an analysis of your own. At the conclusion of your analysis, list some general guidelines to follow when you begin to write exam questions.

11–7   Making Up Sample Test Items

A good way to become aware of the difficulties and complexities of evaluation (as well as to understand different types of tests) is to devise some test questions. Take a chapter or two from the text and compose several kinds of questions—say, three to five multiple-choice, three to five completion, five true-false, a matching question (if the material seems appropriate), three short essay, and one or two long essay questions. Be sure to make up your key as you write the questions. Then ask one or two classmates to take your test. Request that they not only record their answers but also add any critical remarks about the strengths and weaknesses of specific items. Summarize the answers and criticisms and draw up a list of guidelines to follow when you construct classroom examinations.

11–8   Reading a More Complete Analysis of Testing

The discussion of testing in the text is oversimplified. If you would like further information to prepare yourself for this important aspect of teaching, look through several books on the subject in a library and select one or two that strike you as promising. Especially recommended is *Measuring Educational Achievement* (1965) by Robert L. Ebel. In Chapter 1 Ebel discusses "The Need for Better Classroom Tests." In Chapter 3 he describes "How to Plan a Classroom Test." In Chapters 4, 5, and 6 he gives specific suggestions for writing essay, true-false, and multiple-choice test items. Ebel also comments on how to judge the quality of the exams you write (Chapter 9), tells how to perform an item analysis (Chapter 11), and analyzes marks and marking systems (Chapter 13). If you read sections of Ebel's book, or of one or more similar volumes, summarize the points you think will be most valuable when you begin to measure educational achievement on your own.

11–9   Analyzing the Systematic Asking of Questions to Help Students Use Ideas

In *Classroom Questions: What Kinds?* (1966) Norris M. Sanders describes how to write and pose questions which require students to *use* ideas rather than simply remember them. Sanders bases his approach on the taxonomy of educational objectives. The hierarchical nature of learning stressed in the taxonomy is too often ignored, he feels, when questions are asked. Teachers are partial to memory-level questions, and thus restrict students to the bottom of the hierarchy of learning. The memorization of facts should not be an end in itself, but a means to permit the student to interpret ideas, make applications, analyze, and synthesize. Proper use of questions helps the student perform these higher-level operations *as* he answers. In *Classroom Questions: What Kinds?* Sanders devotes a chapter to questions which might be used in testing each of the categories in the taxonomy: memory, translation, interpretation, application, analysis, synthesis, and evaluation. Many examples are offered, and each chapter concludes with questions designed to test the reader's understanding of the discussion. For more on the possibility of using the taxonomy of educational objectives not only to plan lessons but also to make up questions, secure a copy of *Classroom Questions: What Kinds?* (It is an inexpensive paperback.) Outline the ideas you regard as most valuable, perhaps in the form of a personal "handbook" on how to make systematic use of classroom questions.

11–10   Assigning Grades on the Basis of Excerpts from a Grade Book

There are many things to be considered when the time comes to assign final grades. Below are excerpts from a hypothetical grade book. (This exercise was devised by Dr. John G. Safarik of Chico State College, who attempted to include as many complicating factors as possible.) Assume you are the teacher of an eleventh-grade class in Social Studies and are to give final grades on the basis of the information provided below. Final grades are recorded only as "A," "B," "C," "D," "F," or "Inc." (for incomplete). After assigning *your* grades, compare them with those of a fellow student or students —and explain any discrepancies. Or conduct your own analysis by stating the sorts of situations which might lead to complications. In either case, note the implications of your comparison or analysis and perhaps establish some guidelines for minimizing difficulties when final grade time arrives.

	Sem. Gr. Fall	Final Exam	Mid-term II	Mid-term I	Sum Wkly. Quizzes	Av. Gr., Hmwk.	% Hmwk. Comp.	No. Times Absent	I.Q.	Final Grade
Adams, A.	C	44	26	6	81	A	12	8	98	
Has told the teacher of his plan to quit school.										
Baker, C.	A	58	31	10	138	A	100	0	119	
The teacher's daughter.										
Cook, D.		39	20	4	84	D	41	2	90	
On parole from the Youth Authority.										
Davis, R.	B	51	32	8	130	B	97	3	116	
High anxiety all year, took midterm when ill.										
Evans, G.	C	41	27	6	110	C	100	1	100	
Desperately trying to get into scholarship society.										
Ford, H.	D	61	24	7	55	A	8	11	83	
"Bad" boy, sent to office 18 times this year by the teacher.										
Gary, N.	B	55	28	9	125	B	90	2	105	
Some of the kids call her "teacher's pet."										
Hood, B.	C	35	21	6	104	C	70	0	97	
Star player on the baseball team (C avg. req.).										
Ingram, R.	Inc.	63	23	6	141	D	73	3	102	
Owes library fine, not to receive grade until paid.										
Jones, C.	D	24	18	3	61	F	86	2	72	
The school psychologist says she may be mentally retarded.										
Kent, P.	C	52	24	7	106	C	25	5	113	
Works full time, nights, in a local gas station.										
Landis, H.	C	46	22	F	75	D	83	2	96	
Was caught cheating on the first midterm.										
Moore, J.	F	49	24	5	92	C	64	6	87	
Sullen, always marginal conduct with the teacher.										
Norton, C.	C	69	18		76	C	37	1	80	
Entered class in middle of semester with a C.										
Parker, N.	B	47	26	8	106	B	100	0	92	
Absolutely head over heels in love with the teacher.										
Quist, A.	A	55	27	9	120	B	41	7	88	
Blind, has special help from "itinerant" special ed. teacher.										
Radke, L.	B	53	23	8	109	B	59	3	108	
Son of an M.D., he too plans to be an M.D.										

Smith, J.	C	37	21	6	115	C	66	0	93

A social isolate, her only chum is in the ninth grade.

Terry, R.	C	45	26	7	100	C	82	4	106

Son of a member of the school board.

Unger, V.	A	71		11	135	B	81	6	103

Missed midterm due to illness.

Vance, A.	C	54	22	7	91	D	38	1	121

Acts all right at school but arrested and convicted of a felony this year.

Ward, G.	C	43	27	6	96	B	74	6	94

The teacher feels sure he usually just copies someone else's homework.

Ward, M.	C		26	2	112	C	59	5	112

Moved away three weeks before end of semester.

York, C.	B	60	27	9	105	C	100	1	104

A model of good behavior, has never done anything wrong.

Zucker, A.	C	48	26	7	98	C	65	5	107

Parents will take his car away if he doesn't get B or higher.

11–11   Speculating about the Possibility of Schools without Failure

William Glasser is a psychiatrist who has analyzed traditional approaches to education and concluded that American schools cause too many students to fail. How we might reverse this trend is the subject of *Schools Without Failure* (1969). Glasser feels that the first years in school are of crucial importance, and that overemphasis on memorization and grades leads numerous children to be labeled and/or to think of themselves as failures early in their academic careers. His prescription for reform advises "involvement, relevance and thinking." He recommends group discussion as the basic pedagogical method, argues for greater emphasis on having students relate what they learn in school to their lives outside it, and suggests that a grading system in which a student gets either a "Pass" or a "Superior" (but never an "F") be substituted for the usual system. Perhaps because of his medical background, Glasser proposes a simple, definite diagnosis and prescribes simple, definite treatment. For an overview of *one* way schools might attempt to minimize failure, you might read *Schools Without Failure*. Chapter 1 is devoted to a general analysis of the problem, Chapter 6 is a critique of tests and grades, and Chapter 10 consists of Glasser's description of how teachers should use group discussion as *the* main approach to teaching. If you would prefer deeper and more comprehensive analyses of some of the same points Glasser covers, you might read John Holt's observations on failure (*How Children Fail*, 1964), Banesh Hoffmann's critique of grades (*The Tyranny of Testing*, 1962), the discussions of the discovery approach provided by Jerome Bruner

(*Toward a Theory of Instruction,* 1966), Morris L. Bigge (*Learning Theories for Teachers,* 1964), or Herbert A. Thelen (*Education and the Human Quest,* 1960), or the descriptions of the theory and practice of learning for mastery offered by Bloom, Hastings, and Madaus (*Formative and Summative Evaluation of Student Learning,* in preparation). If you read Glasser's book or one of the others, summarize the arguments presented and add your own reactions.

11–12 Devising Your Own Approach to Learning for Mastery

It is difficult to disagree or find fault with the basic point emphasized by John Holt and William Glasser, i.e., that our present approach to education leads many students to experience failure. However, there seem to be limitations to their prescriptions for change. Holt argues for an "intellectual smorgasbord"; Glasser advocates group discussion. Both methods are highly appropriate and effective in certain situations, and you may wish to use them from time to time. It is not likely that you will be able to rely on either technique exclusively, however, because of the organization and administration of public schools in this country. An approach to minimizing the impact of failure which seems to permit greater flexibility is the *learning-for-mastery* concept of John Carroll and Benjamin Bloom, discussed at length in *Formative and Summative Evaluation of Student Learning* (in preparation) by Bloom, Hastings, and Madaus. Even if you are unable to obtain this book, speculate about how you could use some variation of a mastery approach to give more students an opportunity to avoid failure. How might you specify educational objectives and then set about helping your students master them? How might you guide learning experiences so that the difference between good and not-so-good students would be the *amount of time* needed to master material rather than the quality of performance produced within a given period of time? What provisions could you make so that students who did not do adequate work on a first attempt had the opportunity and motivation to try again as opposed to developing a sense of fatalistic resignation? Too many students in American schools *do* experience failure. What kind of plan can you propose so that more students in your classes will feel successful?

Evaluating Achievement and Learning Ability

Key Points

Terminology	Standardized test
	Age-level scale, basal age, ceiling age, deviation I.Q. (Stanford-Binet)
	Verbal Scale score, Performance Scale score (WISC, WAIS)
	Individual test, group test
Sequences and Trends	Maturing of separate intellectual abilities at different ages in same child; also variance among individuals
	Controversy over relative influence of heredity and environment in determining intelligence; new interpretation by Jensen of heredity's role
Criteria	Allowance for measurement errors in interpretation of I.Q. scores
Experiments and Studies	No clear link between I.Q. scores and creativity (Getzels and Jackson)
	Close similarity in intelligence of most identical twins reared apart but some sharp exceptions (Newman, Freeman, and Holzinger)
	Much closer resemblance of foster child's I.Q. to true mother's than to foster parents' (Skodak and Skeels)
	I.Q. correlations: true parent and child +.50, foster parent and child +.20 (Burks and Leahy)
	Limited impact of nursery school programs on I.Q. (Heber)
Concepts	Normal probability curve
	Standard deviation; Z scores, T scores
	Stanines
	Intelligence as a composite of five *operations*, four *contents*, and six *products*, which interact to produce 120 separate abilities (Guilford)
Methodology	Administering standardized achievement tests
	Interpreting scores: grade-equivalent, percentile rank, standard

Chapter Contents

Testing and Organizing Your Knowledge of Key Points in Chapter 12

Terminology

1. The term *standardized* test indicates an important characteristic of one form of evaluation. In the space below explain the quality of standardized tests that makes this term appropriate.

_____

_____

_____

_____

_____

2. A well-informed teacher should have some familiarity with the nature and characteristics of the Stanford-Binet, one of the most highly respected individual tests of intelligence. In the spaces below explain the meaning of the terms *age-level scale, basal age, ceiling age,* and *deviation I.Q.* with reference to the Stanford-Binet.

Age-level scale

_____

_____

_____

_____

Basal age

_____

_____

_____

Ceiling age

_____

_____

_____

Deviation I.Q.

_____

_____

_____

3. Other than the Stanford-Binet, the two most widely used individual tests of intelligence are the WISC and the WAIS. Awareness of what is meant by two types of scores yielded by these tests will assist you to comprehend the basic difference between the Wechsler tests and the Stanford-Binet. In the following spaces explain the meaning and significance of a *verbal score* and a *performance score* on a WISC or WAIS, and then note how these differ from the I.Q. score yielded by the Stanford-Binet.

Verbal score

_____

_____

_____

Performance score

_____

_____

_____

_____

Significance of difference between WISC and S-B scores

_____

_____

_____

_____

_____

_____

4. The Stanford-Binet, the WISC, and the WAIS are individual tests of intelligence. In the spaces below explain what is meant by the term _individual test_ and contrast this with a _group test_.

Individual test

_____

_____

_____

_____

Group test

_____

_____

_____

_____

Trends and Sequences

1. The measurement of intelligence is complicated by the fact that various intellectual abilities appear to mature at different rates in different children. The somewhat unpredictable sequence of development makes it hard to compare I.Q. scores obtained at different age levels. In the following space tell why a less than completely uniform sequence of intellectual development

might make the interpretation of I.Q. scores more complex. (What explanations might you give, for example, if a child's Stanford-Binet I.Q. is 105 at the age of five but 120 at the age of ten?)

_____

_____

_____

_____

_____

_____

2. A controversy in education and psychology centers around the relative impact of heredity and environment on intelligence. Thirty years ago the hereditarians felt they had proved their point. Ten years ago the environmentalists, under the leadership of J. McV. Hunt, believed they had presented evidence to refute the earlier arguments of hereditarians. At present new arguments in favor of heredity are being offered by Arthur Jensen. In the spaces below summarize the current state of the heredity-environment controversy by contrasting Hunt's and Jensen's views.

Hunt's arguments in favor of an environmentalist position

_____

_____

_____

_____

_____

_____

Jensen's arguments in favor of a hereditarian position

_____

_____

_____

_____

_____

_____

Criteria

When you are presented with group test scores reflecting the relative standing of your students on some aspect of intellectual or academic performance, you will want to exercise caution in making use of the information. In the space below describe some situations and conditions which might cause errors of measurement when standardized tests are used.

Situations and conditions which might lead to errors of measurement in standardized test scores

_____

_____

_____

_____

_____

_____

Experiments and Studies

1. Getzels and Jackson studied the relationship between creativity and intelligence, a relationship that has considerable significance for teachers. In the spaces below describe the experimental design and note the general conclusions of the Getzels and Jackson study and comment on the implications of these findings.

Experimental design of Getzels and Jackson study

_____

_____

_____

_____

_____

Conclusions

_____

_____

_____

_____

_____

Implications

_____

_____

_____

_____

_____

_____

2. A large number of studies have been conducted by experimenters interested in the relative impact of heredity and environment on intelligence. In most cases the experimental design features the use of identical twins reared apart (e.g., the Newman, Freeman, and Holzinger study), comparisons between the I.Q.'s of a foster child and his true and foster parents (e.g., the Skodak and Skeels study), or comparisons between the I.Q.'s of foster children and their foster parents and true children and true parents (e.g., the Burks or Leahy study). In the spaces below describe the general results of each study.

Identical twins reared apart (Newman, Freeman, and Holzinger)

_____

_____

_____

_____

Comparisons between I.Q.'s of a foster child and his true and foster parents (Skodak and Skeels)

_____

_____

_____

Comparisons between the I.Q.'s of foster children and parents and true children and parents (Burks or Leahy)

_____

_____

_____

_____

3. Approximately thirty follow-up studies of the impact of Head Start and similar preschool programs have been carried out in the last few years. Heber has summarized the results of these investigations. In the space below describe the general conclusions offered by Heber after he analyzed the studies.

_____

_____

_____

_____

_____

_____

Concepts

1. A widely used (and frequently misunderstood) concept in education and psychology is the *normal probability curve*. Since you are almost sure to encounter this concept—or scores derived from or based on it—you should be able to draw a normal probability curve and explain what it represents. Use the spaces below.

Drawing of a normal probability curve

_____

What this diagram represents

_____

_____

_____

_____

_____

_____

2. When the normal probability curve is used in conjunction with the *standard deviation*, it is possible to make many inferences about a set of test scores. In the spaces below give a brief description of what the standard deviation is and a general explanation of what it is used for.

Description of standard deviation

_____

_____

_____

_____

_____

What SD is used for

_____

_____

_____

_____

_____

3. Once a standard deviation is calculated, it is possible to derive two different kinds of scores—Z scores and T scores. In the spaces below explain each of these scores.

Explanation of a Z score

_____

_____

_____

_____

Explanation of a T score (including reasons a T score may be easier to use)

_____

_____

_____

_____

4. An additional score which can be derived from a normal probability curve is a *stanine* score. In the spaces below diagram and explain stanines.

Diagram of stanine scores

_____

Explanation of stanine scores

_____

_____

_____

_____

5. To test your ability to apply the information you have just given regarding the standard deviation, Z scores, T scores, and stanines, answer the questions below.

Suppose you get a set of test scores for two different classes. Class A has a mean of 100 and a standard deviation of 10. Class B has a mean of 100 and a standard deviation of 20. (Assume both distributions are close to normal.)

What is the Z score of a student in Class A who earns a raw score of 110?

_____

What is the Z score of a student in Class B who earns a raw score of 110?

_____

What is the T score of a student in Class A who earns a raw score of 80?

_____

What is the T score of a student in Class B who earns a raw score of 80?

_____

To clarify the relationship between these two sets of scores and also to check on your answers, indicate the mean for Class A and for Class B at the center point of the two following lines. Then with a ruler mark off three standard deviations on either side of the mean. (Allow one-sixteenth of an inch for two points; e.g., a score of 110 will be five-sixteenths from the mean.) Note the score which will fall under each standard deviation point (e.g., insert *1 SD* and also the number *110* under the mark which is five-sixteenths to the right of the mean).

Class A

_____ | _____

Class B

_____ | _____

If you interpret your answers to the questions above with reference to these diagrams, you will get feedback as to the accuracy of your computation. You will also appreciate the significance of a difference between standard deviations. The average score for Class A and Class B is the same, but note the difference between the lowest and highest scores for distributions which have different standard deviations.

Next, draw a normal curve over each of the base lines for Class A and Class B and insert the rough percentage of cases you would expect to find within each standard deviation unit. (It will be 34 percent between the mean and ±1 SD, 14 percent between ±1 SD and ±2 SD, and 2 percent between ±2 SD and ±3 SD. If this is not clear, refer to Figure 12–1, page 418 of the text.) Now that you have recorded this information, you can estimate the percentage of cases which fall below a given student simply by examining the diagram. To demonstrate the procedure to yourself, answer the questions below.

What is the percentage of cases falling below a student who earned a score of 80 in Class A?_____

What is the percentage of cases falling below a student who earned a score of 80 in Class B?_____

What is the percentage of cases falling below a student who earned a score of 110 in Class A?_____

What is the percentage of cases falling below a student who earned a score of 110 in Class B?_____

The implications of the difference between a small and large SD should be more apparent to you now than they were previously. One other thing should be evident. Unless you know the formula for calculating percentile ranks, you had to "guess" at the percentage of cases which fall below the student who earned a score of 110 in Class B since his is the only score given in these problems which does not land exactly on a standard deviation point. Perhaps you "assigned" this person a percentile rank by simply dividing the percentage of cases within one standard deviation above the mean in half and adding that to 50. Was it proper to do this? If not, why not? Indicate your answer in the space below. (If you are unable to answer this question, refer to Figure 12–2, page 421 in the text.)

_____

_____

_____

_____

In making inferences about the information you derived in answering the preceding questions, you were operating under the implied assumption that the scores for the two classes were distributed in an essentially normal manner. Suppose both distributions had been *skewed,* with a disproportionate number of high or low scores at one end of the distribution; or suppose three or four scores were abnormally high (or low). Is it proper to make inferences about relative position with reference to a normal curve if the actual distribution is abnormal? If not, why not?

_____

_____

_____

_____

One last set of questions on the use of the normal curve has to do with scores on various standardized tests. Perhaps you are unfamiliar with the relative position of different I.Q. scores. If you will mark off the standard deviation units for the WISC on the following base line (remember that the WISC has an SD of 15), then draw a normal curve and insert the percentages to be found within each standard deviation above and below the mean, you will quickly be able to determine the position of a student, for example, who earns an I.Q. of 85 as compared with one who earns an I.Q. of 130. (The same diagram can be used in interpreting scores on the WAIS or the Stanford-Binet.)

_____ | _____

6. J. P. Guilford has proposed a conception of intelligence which suggests that there are 120 separate mental abilities. These abilities fall into three groups. One group having special significance for teachers consists of five intellectual *operations*. Since awareness of these operations may assist you in evaluating students, you should be able to list and describe them and note how knowledge of the different types of intelligence might be of value to a teacher. Use the space below.

Description of Guilford's five intellectual operations

a. _____

_____

_____

b. _____

_____

_____

c. _____

_____

_____

d. _____

_____

_____

e. _____

_____

_____

Significance of Guilford's concept that there are different types of intelligence

_____

_____

_____

_____

Methodology

1. The way standardized tests are administered may be of considerable importance. In the space below outline three general guidelines for administering standardized tests so as to make them as valid and reliable as possible.

a. _____

_____

b. _____

_____

c. _____

_____

2. It is quite likely that you will have to interpret scores on standardized tests. In the spaces below describe and/or demonstrate the meaning and use of the types of scores noted.

Grade-equivalent scores

_____

_____

_____

Percentile ranks

_____

_____

_____

Stanines

_____

_____

_____

_____

3. To demonstrate your ability actually to interpret the types of scores you just described, refer to Figure 12–4 on page 423 of the text and provide the information requested below.

Taking into account that the grade placement of James Harris at the time he was tested was 2.8, what does his *grade score* for Paragraph Meaning indicate?

_____

_____

_____

Assume that Mr. and Mrs. Harris come to a parent-teacher conference and ask you to explain the *percentile rank* Jimmy earned on Word Meaning. (They have the impression that he flunked that part of the test.) How would you explain Jimmy's percentile rank on Word Meaning to his parents?

_____

_____

_____

_____

What does Jimmy's *stanine* placement for Arithmetic Computation indicate?

_____

_____

_____

_____

Suggestions for Further Reading, Thinking, and Discussion

12–1   Analyzing Your Experiences with Standardized Tests

Do you recall taking a standardized test that seemed exceptionally well or badly administered? (For example, did you ever have a teacher who seemed confused about how to proceed or who made a great show of using a stop-watch or the like?) Do you recall any situation in which the scores you received on a standardized test had undesirable repercussions? (For example, did you ever have a teacher who seemed to evaluate you more in terms of your test profile than on the basis of what you considered your actual performance? Did you find your previously high self-confidence shaken by a low test score and come to doubt your ability to do good work?) After describing any negative or positive experiences you have had with standardized tests, draw a "moral" for each experience.

12–2   Taking an Individual Test of Intelligence

If you wonder what it is like to take an individual test of intelligence, you might check on the possibility that a teacher of a course in individual testing needs subjects for practice purposes. (In most courses of this type, each student is required to give several tests under practice conditions.) Look in a class schedule for a course in psychology or education designated Individual Testing, Practicum in Testing, or something similar. Contact the instructor and ask him whether he wants subjects. If you do find yourself acting as guinea pig, jot down your reactions to the test immediately after you take it. Would you feel comfortable about having the score used to determine whether you would be admitted to some program or would qualify for a promotion? Did the test seem to provide an adequate sample of your intelligence? Were the kinds of questions appropriate for *your* conception of intelligence? Record your reactions and comment on the implications.

12–3   Evaluating a Standardized Test

In most school systems the selection and use of standardized tests is supervised by a specialist in testing. It is possible, however, that you will have to make your own evaluation of a test or several alternate tests. To find out the kinds of information available for evaluating standardized tests, examine the most recent edition of the *Mental Measurements Yearbooks* edited by O. K. Buros, or look for a recent copy of the *Review of Educational Research,* published by the American Educational Research Association. Issues of this journal entitled "Psychological Tests and Their Uses," "Educational Tests and Their Uses," and "Methods of Research and Appraisal in Education" contain references to new tests and to research findings with old tests. Select two or more tests designed for the same general purpose (by examining the catalogs of test publishers or obtaining sample copies from a test library), and compare them on the basis of the following factors:

Title

Year of publication

Purpose as described by test publisher

Group to which applicable

Cost of test booklets

Cost of answer sheets

Time required

Types of scores

Evidence of validity: size and nature of standardization group, evidence regarding relationship of scores on given test to scores on other tests, etc.

Evidence of reliability: method of estimating consistency of scores, size and nature of sample

Estimate of ease of administration, clarity of instructions, etc.

Kinds of scores and how reported

Comments of reviewers in *Mental Measurements Yearbook* and/or *Review of Educational Research*

After making your comparison, indicate which test you prefer and explain your reasons why.

12–4 Evaluating the Significance of Guilford's Five Mental Operations

To gain greater insight into J. P. Guilford's factors of intelligence, you might speculate about the significance of his five mental operations—cognition, memory, convergent production, divergent production, and evaluation. Guilford suggests that most forms of evaluation place too much emphasis on only one or two of these operations. As you consider making up tests of your own, give some thought to this point. Were many of the tests you have taken as a student designed to tap only one or two of the operations described by Guilford? Did this have a detrimental effect—and if so, how did it influence you in an undesirable way? How might you avoid or minimize the harmful effects of tests which measure only a limited type of intellectual ability?

12–5 Examining the Pros and Cons of Assessing Creative Potential

A number of tests to measure creative potential have been devised, primarily because studies such as those of Getzels and Jackson indicate that measures of intelligence do not necessarily reflect mental operations associated with creativity. Taking into account different types of intelligence is to be desired as a means for broadening the assessment of abilities, but it is possible that a creativity score *causes* just as many problems as it eliminates. Suppose, for example, that the students in your classes were given a test of creativity and the scores were reported to you. What would you do with them? Would you place children with high scores in special groups or give them special opportunities to demonstrate their ability? Would you evaluate assignments with reference to the scores—i.e., look more carefully for signs of creativity in the work of those who earned high scores? Would you distrust your own judgment that the work of a pupil was highly creative if you knew he had a low score on the test? Or would you be better off simply encouraging *all* pupils to be as creative as possible and not being concerned about an estimate of creative potential, on the assumption that creativity flourishes when there are abundant opportunities for each person to express himself in his own way? If you are intrigued by the question of the use or abuse of measures of creativity, record your observations and perhaps list some guidelines for encouraging free expression which you might apply in your classes.

12–6   Comparing the Views of Jensen and His Critics

It may be difficult to make up your mind regarding the relative influence of heredity and environment on intelligence, in which case you are urged to read Arthur Jensen's article "How Much Can We Boost IQ and Scholastic Achievement?" in the Winter, 1969, issue of the *Harvard Educational Review*. This article is essentially a "reply" to the arguments presented by J. McV. Hunt in his *Intelligence and Experience*. (You are reminded that Hunt suggested that we ought to be able to raise I.Q.'s by an average of thirty points, and that he is one of the chief advisers to the Head Start program.) The Spring, 1969, issue of the *Harvard Educational Review* consists of criticisms of the Jensen article, and the Summer, 1969, issue presents Jensen's reply to the critics. If you are unable to find the journal, look for the articles in book form under the title *Environment, Heredity and Intelligence*. To form your own opinions on the Jensen controversy, read the views of Jensen and his critics and record your conclusions.

Part Six / Individual Differences and Adjustment

STUDY GUIDE

Teaching Exceptional
Students

Key Points

Classifications

Custodial, trainable, and educable levels of mental retardation

Criteria

Mental retardation: subaverage general intellectual functioning associated with
  impaired adaptive behavior (A.A.M.D. definition)
Characteristics of the trainable and the educable mentally retarded
Detecting visual handicaps
Detecting hearing handicaps

**Experiments
and Studies**

Gain in I.Q. for culturally deprived MR's but not for organically disabled MR's as
  result of intensive preschooling (Kirk)
Self-sufficiency of EMR graduates in later life (Charles)
No corroboration of Doman-Delacato's neurological organization theory, or
  patterning, by controlled study (Robbins)
Superior behavior and adjustment of students early identified as intellectually
  gifted (Terman and Oden)

Concepts

Regression toward the mean
Low convulsive threshold as explanation of epilepsy

Methodology

Teaching slow learners
Teaching the visually handicapped
Teaching pupils with impaired speech

Teaching rapid learners
Teaching the hard of hearing
Teaching and dealing with epileptics

Chapter Contents

Testing and Organizing Your Knowledge of Key Points in Chapter 13

Classifications

In order to communicate with each other more effectively, educators and psychologists use classification schemes of various kinds when referring to levels of intelligence. The most common classification of types of mentally retarded persons includes the terms *custodial, trainable,* and *educable.* Since you will probably encounter these terms in articles or in conversations, you should be aware of the levels of intelligence they indicate. In the spaces below indicate the I.Q. range, the approximate mental age range, and the approximate frequency of children classified under each heading.

	I.Q. Range	*Approximate MA Range*	*Approximate Frequency*
Custodial			
Trainable			
Educable			

Criteria

1. The American Association on Mental Deficiency definition of mental retardation emphasizes three major factors in the identification of those who are below average in intelligence. The definition indicates what is meant by *subaverage* and points to impairment in certain types of *adaptive behavior*. In the spaces below define the term *subaverage* and explain three types of adaptive behavior which might be used as criteria for assessing subaverage functioning.

Definition of *subaverage*

_____

_____

_____

Types of adaptive behavior which are considered in the A.A.M.D. definition of mental retardation

a. _____

_____

_____

b. _____

_____

_____

c. _____

_____

_____

2. Students who are mentally retarded are often placed in special classes. The characteristics of those who are classified as *trainable* and *educable* MR's can serve as criteria for evaluating general levels of functioning. In the spaces below summarize some traits of students typically found in trainable and educable classes.

Characteristics of trainable MR's

_____

_____

_____

_____

Characteristics of educable MR's

_____

_____

_____

_____

3. Students who have visual and hearing problems often manifest certain types of behavior which might be used as criteria for evaluating the possibility of those handicaps. In the spaces below note four types of behavior which might indicate visual or hearing problems.

Symptoms of visual problems

a. _____

_____

b. _____

_____

c. _____

_____

d. _____

_____

Symptoms of hearing problems

a. _____

_____

b. _____

_____

c. _____

_____

d. _____

_____

Experiments

1. A carefully controlled study of special education of mentally retarded children was conducted by Samuel Kirk. In the following spaces describe the study's design and results and comment on the implications.

Experimental design of Kirk study

_____

_____

_____

_____

Results of study

_____

_____

_____

_____

Implications of results

_____

_____

_____

_____

2. Doman and Delacato have proposed a theory of intelligence which leads to the belief that certain types of physical exercise can "recirculate" brain cells. One of the few well-controlled studies designed to test this theory —and the effectiveness of the patterning technique based on the theory— was conducted by Melvyn Robbins. In the following spaces describe the experimental design of the Robbins study, note the results, and comment on the implications of the results.

Experimental design of Robbins study

_____

_____

_____

_____

_____

Results of study

_____

_____

_____

_____

Implications

_____

_____

_____

_____

_____

3. In a follow-up study, W. A. Charles obtained information on the mid-life behavior and adjustment of graduates of classes for the educable mentally retarded. In the space below summarize the results of this survey.

_____

_____

_____

_____

_____

4. Lewis Terman and Melita Oden investigated the mid-life behavior and adjustment of individuals who had been identified as intellectually gifted early in life. In the space below summarize the general conclusions of this survey.

_____

_____

_____

_____

Concepts

1. A factor which complicates estimates (and reestimates) of intelligence is *regression toward the mean*. In the following space explain and give an example of two ways in which regression toward the mean might lead to dif-

ferent estimates of the intelligence of individuals (or their offspring) who are at either extreme of a distribution of I.Q. scores.

a. _____

_____

_____

_____

b. _____

_____

_____

_____

2. In discussions of causes of epileptic seizures, the concept of a *low convulsive threshold* is often mentioned. In the space below explain what is meant by this term.

_____

_____

_____

_____

Methodology

1. Regardless of the grade level or subject matter you teach, some of your students will learn at a slower rate than others. If slow learners are considerably below the level of their classmates, you may wish to try variations of methods of instruction used in classes for the educable mentally retarded. In the following space note three teaching techniques you might use with slow learners, particularly techniques for helping them achieve some of the goals typically emphasized in EMR classes.

a. _____

_____

_____

b. _____

_____

_____

c. _____

_____

_____

2. Regardless of the grade level or subject matter you teach, you will have some students who learn more easily and quickly than others. If rapid learners are considerably above the level of their classmates, you may find special types of instruction helpful. In the space below note three pedagogical techniques you might use with students who learn faster than the average pupil.

a. _____

_____

_____

b. _____

_____

_____

c. _____

_____

_____

3. From time to time you may be asked to teach a pupil who has a visual or hearing handicap. In the spaces below give two general guidelines for teaching each type of student.

Guidelines to follow in teaching a student with a visual handicap

a. _____

_____

b. _____

_____

Guidelines to follow in teaching a student with a hearing handicap

a. _____

_____

b. _____

_____

4. Some students develop speech problems, the most disturbing of which is stuttering. Since this can cause tension and embarrassment for the child with the problem—as well as for his classmates and teacher—you will do well to think ahead to how you might deal with it. In the space below state three general guidelines to follow if one of your students is bothered by stuttering.

a. _____

_____

b. _____

_____

c. _____

_____

5. One of the most common but least understood neurological disorders is epilepsy. Because this condition is accompanied by so much emotional involvement and misinformation, children subject to epileptic seizures are not always identified as such. Thus your first awareness that you have an epileptic in class may come as a result of a grand mal seizure. It will be to your advantage to plan what to do if a pupil suddenly has an epileptic attack. In the space below note three guidelines for handling such a situation.

a. _____

_____

b. _____

_____

c. _____

_____

Suggestions for Further Reading, Thinking, and Discussion

13–1   Observing in a Special Class

In case you have ever considered becoming a teacher of a special class of some kind, you might ask your instructor to help you make arrangements to visit such a classroom. Most large school districts have TMR and EMR classes, as well as separate classes for the blind and partially sighted, for the deaf and hard of hearing, and for children with cerebral palsy and related conditions. Following your observation, describe the characteristics of the pupils which seemed most noticeable or record your general reactions.

13-2 Reading a More Detailed Account of Mental Retardation

If you are interested in mental retardation, you might wish to do some further reading to supplement the brief analysis in the text. You will find a concise discussion of mental retardation with emphasis on teaching in *The Mentally Retarded Child in the Classroom* (1965) by Marion J. Erickson. For a comprehensive account of the causes of mental retardation and a penetrating analysis of ramifications of retardation, look for *The Mentally Retarded Child* (1965) by Halbert B. Robinson and Nancy M. Robinson. You might also browse through books in the appropriate section of a library. If you read either of the books noted above or one you find on your own, summarize points you think might be of value to you later on.

13-3 Sampling Suggestions for Teaching Rapid Learners

Since it is widely believed that American schools do not pay sufficient attention to exceptionally bright students, perhaps you will want more information on teaching the gifted. *Gifted Children in the Classroom* (1965) by E. Paul Torrance, *Teaching the Gifted Child* (1964) by James J. Gallagher, and *Curriculum Planning for the Gifted* (1961) edited by Louis A. Fliegler are especially recommended, although you will probably find several other books on the subject in any college library. If you do further reading about teaching rapid learners, summarize points you think might serve as guidelines when you begin to teach.

13-4 Reading More Detailed Accounts of Handicapped Children

If you are interested in teaching children with specific types of handicaps, you might wish to do further reading. For a brief account of visual, hearing, speech, and other problems, look up a text on the exceptional child. *Exceptional Children in the Schools* (1963) by Lloyd Dunn is particularly recommended, but you will probably find several similar books in a college library. For more detail on a specific handicap, consult a teacher of a special class or look in a library card catalog. A concise, inexpensive source of ideas for teaching all types of exceptional children is *Helping Children with Special Needs* (1956) by DeHaan and Kough. Select points from your reading which impress you as being important and summarize the information for future reference.

13–5   Speculating about Life in a Meritocracy

Numerous arguments have been presented in favor of merit pay or merit advancement, each individual's career depending on objective assessment of his abilities. It is averred that the most capable people should be in positions of influence, and the less capable should hold jobs appropriate to their lower level of functioning. In many respects, our society is already moving in this direction, since it is very common for organizations to use tests to decide among candidates for a given job. The English sociologist Michael Young has written a fascinating interpretation of what might happen if a society became a pure meritocracy. He emphasizes the difficulties that may arise if overconcern with measurement of abilities gets out of hand. You are urged to read *The Rise of the Meritocracy* (1959). Do you think events would occur in the manner postulated by Young? If not, note your own speculations. You might also attempt to relate the observations of Young to special education. Are there points made in *The Rise of the Meritocracy* which highlight possible dangers of too much identification, segregation, and education of individuals who are either above or below average?

13–6   Reacting to a Fictional Account of the "Manipulation" of a Genius

John Hersey found himself disturbed by the extreme reaction of some Americans to the launching of Sputnik. In many areas an all-out campaign was initiated to identify brilliant children and then offer them a speeded-up curriculum in an effort to produce "instant scientists." In his novel *The Child Buyer* (1960), Hersey describes what might have occurred if this tendency had gone too far. While Hersey's account is exaggerated, it does emphasize certain dangers involved in any attempt to *force* growth. If you have ever wondered about the possible disadvantages of attempting to "push" a child prodigy in a desired direction, you will enjoy reading this novel. Record your reactions.

Teaching to Encourage
Need Gratification

Key Points

Classifications
Determinants of personality: constitutional, group membership, role, situational (Murray and Kluckhohn)
Deficiency and growth needs (Maslow)

Criteria
Symptoms of maladjustment: depression, unsocialness, fearfulness, suspiciousness, persistent patterns of behavior, extreme or inappropriate reactions, lack of contact with reality, compulsive behavior

Studies
Opposite judgment of teachers and therapists regarding relative seriousness of misconduct and withdrawal (Wickman)

Concepts
Hierarchy of needs (Maslow)
Behavior as a continual series of choices between safety and growth (Maslow)
The adjustment process as depicted by diagram derived from Lewin
Defense mechanisms: rationalization, identification, compensation
Problems confronting the teacher-psychotherapist
Nondirective, or client-centered, therapy (Rogers)
Sensitivity training (based on principles of client-centered therapy)
Educational engineering and behavior modification (Hewett)

Principles
Aiding students' need gratification by fostering a sense of safety, belongingness, and esteem and by making growth choices attractive (Maslow)

Theories
Need gratification (Maslow)

Methodology
Techniques for sympathetic listening (based on nondirective therapy methods)
Using programmed learning (e.g., Work Record Cards) to overcome learning blocks
Using the discovery approach to help students cope with learning blocks

210

Chapter Contents

Testing and Organizing Your Knowledge of Key Points In Chapter 14

Classifications

1. In order to understand anything as complex as personality, it is necessary to classify related traits in some way. One widely used classification scheme has been proposed by Henry A. Murray and Clyde Kluckhohn. In the following space describe and give an example of the four types of personality determinants noted by Murray and Kluckhohn.

a. _____

_____

_____

b. _____

_____

_____

c. _____

_____

_____

_____

d. _____

_____

_____

_____

2. In Chapter 9 Abraham H. Maslow's hierarchy of needs was described to help you understand why students respond to learning situations in different ways. In Chapter 14 the theory of need gratification is offered as a frame of reference for understanding behavior in general. A key aspect of Maslow's theory is the distinction he makes between *deficiency* and *growth* needs. In the spaces below describe what he means by each type of need, give an example of each, and comment on how awareness of the difference between the two types of needs might assist you in understanding student behavior.

Description and example of a deficiency need

_____

_____

_____

_____

_____

_____

_____

Description and example of a growth need

_____

_____

_____

_____

_____

_____

How knowledge of differences between growth and deficiency needs could be used in understanding behavior

_____

_____

_____

_____

_____

_____

_____

_____

_____

Criteria

All human beings occasionally manifest undesirable behavior. But if a person persists in certain forms of behavior, he may be experiencing especially difficult problems of adjustment. As a teacher you will be continually observing your students as a matter of course. If you are aware of behavior which indicates difficulties in adjustment, you may be able to recognize a problem before it becomes too serious, and arrange for assistance. In the space below describe four patterns of behavior which might be used as criteria to determine whether some pupils are experiencing substantial difficulties in satisfying their needs.

1. _____

_____

2. _____

_____

3. _____

_____

4. _____

_____

Studies

E. K. Wickman carried out a classic study comparing the types of student problem behavior rated most serious by teachers with those rated most serious by psychotherapists. In the spaces below summarize his conclusions and their significance as far as analyzing symptoms of behavior is concerned.

Conclusions of Wickman Study

_____

_____

_____

_____

Significance of conclusions

_____

_____

_____

_____

_____

Concepts

1. In addition to distinguishing between deficiency and growth needs, Maslow conceptualizes behavior as a never-ending series of choices between safety and growth. In the spaces below explain (perhaps by a diagram) this concept and then note guidelines for encouraging students to select growth choices.

Explanation and/or illustration of behavior as a choice between safety and growth

_____

_____

_____

_____

_____

Guidelines for encouraging growth choices

a. _____

_____

_____

_____

b. _____

_____

_____

_____

2. A different way of thinking of the nature of adjustment is evident in a diagram based on the ideas of Kurt Lewin. In the space below draw and explain a diagram showing how achievement of a goal may be thwarted. (What are three possible choices a person might make in such a situation?)

3. When a person makes a safety choice or chooses a substitute goal, he may not gain complete satisfaction of a need. He may then feel driven to compensate for this state of affairs by resorting to one or more *defense mechanisms*. In the space below explain and give an example of how a person might turn to a defense mechanism when a basic need is insufficiently satisfied.

_____

_____

_____

_____

_____

4. Carl Rogers developed the technique of *nondirective* (or client-centered) *therapy* because he believed that traditional approaches to therapy had serious limitations. Recently he has expanded his nondirective conception to education. Traditional approaches to education suffer, he argues, from the same limitations as traditional therapies. In the spaces below explain the main idea of nondirective therapy, then relate this concept to Rogers's view of education—a view which emphasizes variations of sensitivity training.

Rationale of nondirective therapy

_____

_____

_____

_____

_____

Explanation of "nondirective education" with emphasis on sensitivity training

_____

_____

_____

_____

_____

5. A sensitivity-training approach to education may cause conflicts on account of the different roles of teachers and psychotherapists. In the spaces below note three types of conflict that might arise if you try to function as a teacher *and* a therapist (or leader of sensitivity training sessions) at the same time.

a. _____

_____

b. _____

_____

c. _____

_____

Methodology

1. Acceptance of Maslow's distinction between deficit and growth needs makes possible the kind of teaching that helps students satisfy the deficit needs for safety, belongingness, and esteem. (When these needs are satisfied, students are more likely to be capable of self-actualization.) In the spaces below give two general guidelines for assisting your students to satisfy each of the deficit needs noted.

Guidelines for satisfying the need for safety

a. _____

_____

b. _____

_____

Guidelines for satisfying the need for belongingness

a. _____

_____

b. _____

_____

Guidelines for satisfying the need for esteem

a. _____

_____

b. _____

_____

2. In most circumstances a student who exhibits symptoms of difficulties in adjustment should be referred to a trained counselor. Sometimes, however, you will be almost forced to act as a temporary "therapist." In the space below give three general guidelines for use in this situation.

a. _____

_____

b. _____

_____

c. _____

_____

3. Some students have problems of adjustment that interfere with their ability to learn. Techniques for working with such educationally handicapped pupils have been developed by associationists and by field theorists. In the space below describe how you might use techniques of programmed instruction (including the Work Record Card) similar to those evolved by Frank M. Hewett in assisting students with learning blocks.

_____

_____

_____

_____

_____

_____

_____

In the space below describe three general guidelines for using a discovery approach (such as Jerome Bruner's) to combat learning blocks.

a._____

_____

_____

b._____

_____

_____

c._____

_____

_____

Suggestions for Further Reading, Thinking, and Discussion

14–1   Speculating about the Complexity of Personality

You may gain fuller appreciation of the complexity of personality if you speculate about factors which influence behavior. The first part of *Personality in Nature, Society and Culture* (1948) by Murray and Kluckhohn has a complete description of the various determinants of personality development.

You might take this section—or the suggestions offered in Chapter 3 of *Lives in Progress* (1966) by Robert W. White, which includes information on methods and also notes some precautions—and "analyze" either yourself or a close acquaintance. Do your best to make a comprehensive list of all the factors which led to the development of personality, then comment on your reactions to this attempt to gain awareness of the depth and complexity of individuality.

14–2   Sampling Some of Maslow's Views on Adjustment

If you did not do additional reading about Abraham H. Maslow's theory of need gratification earlier (in connection with motivation), you may wish to sample *Toward a a Psychology of Being* (2nd ed., 1968) after thinking about the dynamics of adjustment. In Part I of this book Maslow describes the basic rationale of his theory. In Part II he explains the differences between deficiency motivation and growth motivation. Part VI is devoted to "Some Basic Propositions of a Growth and Self-Actualization Psychology." For a fairly definite set of guidelines for helping your students become self-actualizers, read at least these parts of Maslow's book and note your reactions for future reference.

14–3   Drawing a Diagram of Your Own Behavior

Greater understanding of the diagrams of adjustment depicted in Chapter 14 will be possible if you try a pictorial representation of some of your own behavior. First, draw a diagram of a choice situation you have encountered recently. Analyze your feelings with regard to the situation and classify your final choice as one of safety or growth. Then ask yourself whether you made your decision because of the balance between dangers and attractions as depicted in the diagram on page 500 of the text. Next, speculate about situations centered around a specific goal (e.g., earning an "A" in some course, making the varsity in a certain sport, attracting the attention of a member of the opposite sex, being elected to an office). Did you sometimes achieve the exact goal you sought? What were your feelings when this occurred? Did you sometimes find it necessary to divert your attention to a substitute goal? How did you feel about that? Finally, can you recall being so completely thwarted by your inability to achieve the goal that you avoided the situation completely? What was your inner response on that occasion? Could someone else (e.g., a teacher) have helped you deal with the frustrating situations? Note your reactions to the situations described and comment on the implications of your reactions.

14–4   Describing Your Defense Mechanisms

Abraham Maslow estimates that only one out of a hundred people is a self-actualizer. Since consistent satisfaction of needs is so rare, almost everyone resorts to defense mechanisms from time to time. (Even the best self-actualizer probably rationalizes a bit now and then.) You may become more alert to the nature and impact of defense mechanisms by analyzing your own use of them. Think about your recent behavior and pick out at least one instance of rationalizing, of gaining satisfaction by identifying with others, or of engaging in an activity as a means of compensating for lack of achievement in another activity. Perhaps this will increase your sympathy for and understanding of these forms of behavior in your students.

14–5   Sampling "Lives in Progress"

In *Lives in Progress* (1966), Robert W. White describes the various factors which influence personality by means of three extremely detailed case histories. His analysis of the forces that determine personality uses a different frame of reference from that offered by Murray and Kluckhohn. White shares many of the views of Maslow, notably the convictions that a person "is himself a center of energy and an active agent in changing his material and human surroundings" (page iv), that it is important to stress natural growth and constructive activity, and that much can be gained by studying *normal* people. The three case histories—of a physician and scientist, a businessman, and a housewife and social worker—illustrate this last point. The descriptions provide a good deal of insight into personality and behavior. If you think you would enjoy a comprehensive analysis of a life in progress, read at least one of the case histories in White's book and sample his general analysis of factors that influence personality. Chapter 4 is devoted to social forces, Chapter 6 to biological roots, and Chapter 8 to the psychodynamics of development. The final chapter, "Natural Growth During Young Adulthood," contains observations you might find helpful in your own continuous personal growth and constructive activity. Outline the points made by White and add your own reactions.

14–6   Sampling Rogers's Views on Behavior, Therapy, and Education

Carl Rogers developed the technique of client-centered therapy twenty years ago and has since applied the same basic idea of growth of the self to other aspects of living, including education. For a concise description of Rogers's philosophy, look for "Learning to Be Free," an essay in *Conflict and*

Creativity (1963) edited by Farber and Wilson and also in *Person to Person: The Problem of Being Human* (1967) by Rogers and Stevens. The latter volume includes three more essays by Rogers, as well as related discussions by others who share his philosophy. Since sensitivity training and related techniques are derived from nondirective therapy, you may wish to sample some of the observations of Rogers. Read one or more sections in either of the books noted above, summarize the points made, and add your own reactions.

14–7   Participating in or Finding Out about an Encounter Group

If you are curious about sensitivity training and want to do more than read about it, you might look for someone who has participated in an encounter group or join one yourself. (Campus bulletin boards often have notices announcing encounter groups of one kind or another.) Whether you get first-hand or secondhand information, note your reactions and comment on the possible implications of applying variations of sensitivity training to education.

14–8   Reading about Sensitivity and Awareness in the Classroom

Clark Moustakas has written a book on teaching which combines many of Rogers's ideas with those of Maslow. Some quite specific suggestions for using sensitivity-training techniques in the classroom appear in *The Authentic Teacher* (1966). In this book Moustakas makes general observations on his philosophy of teaching and suggests how this philosophy might be put into practice in the kindergarten (Chapter 4), at the early elementary-grade level (Chapter 5), in the later elementary grades (Chapter 6), and in high school (Chapter 7). If you think you would like to consider some variation of the sensitivity-training approach in your classes, sample the ideas of Moustakas and note those which strike you as most promising.

14–9   Reading a More Complete Discussion of Adjustment

The brief treatment of adjustment presented in Chapter 14 may entice you to browse through *Mental Hygiene in Teaching* (2nd ed., 1959) by Redl and Wattenberg. This exceptionally good book covers almost every aspect of adjustment likely to be of concern to teachers. (There are extended sections on classroom applications and special problems as well as general background information.) For a more comprehensive and theoretical discussion of this aspect of psychology, *The Psychology of Adjustment* (1956) by Shaffer and Shoben is recommended. If you read sections of either of these books, state the points that strike you as being of potential value to the new teacher.

14–10   Tutoring a Student with a Learning Problem

Many campuses now have educational programs providing tutors for pupils with learning problems. (CAVE—Community Action Volunteers for Education—is an example.) If such a program exists at your college, you might volunteer to serve as a tutor. Depending on the nature of the learning problem, the age of the pupil, and the subject matter—not to mention your own philosophy of education—you will perhaps use some of the techniques developed by Frank Hewett in his educational engineering approach and/or those suggested by Jerome Bruner. If you try either programmed techniques or a discovery approach (or use both methods), describe your experiences and summarize your reactions for future reference.

14–11   Speculating about Differences Between Teaching and Therapy

Fantasy and Feeling in Education (1968) by Richard M. Jones was called to your attention earlier in connection with Jerome Bruner's suggestions for teaching social studies. Jones's major point is that Bruner emphasizes the cognitive side of learning at the expense of imagination and emotion. Jones describes techniques teachers might use in introducing more fantasy and feeling into learning. At first glance, this would seem to be essentially the position of those who advocate sensitivity training. However, in urging teachers to place greater stress on the affective side of learning, Jones discusses some basic differences between teaching and therapy. He argues that students go to school to be taught—not treated—and adds, "If the confrontation of emotions in classrooms is not made in the primary interests of achieving instructional objectives, both the means and ends may suffer" (p. 161). If you are interested in attempting any sort of sensitivity-training approach to teaching, consider carefully Jones's comments about the differences between therapy and teaching. For example, you might evaluate Carl Rogers's suggestions regarding an approach to education derived from nondirective therapy with reference to the ideas Jones develops in his book. Or simply note your reactions to the points made by Jones. Does he convince you that imagination and emotion should be stressed more in learning, but that it is unwise for a teacher to use a primarily therapeutic approach in attempting to do this?

14–12   Reading a Case History Which Illustrates the Process of Adjustment and the Techniques of Therapy

A great deal of insight into the dynamics of adjustment and the nature of psychotherapy can be gained by reading a detailed case history. One highly regarded study is *Dibs: In Search of Self* (1964) by Virginia Axline. This book will acquaint you with the factors which caused a child to develop serious problems of adjustment and reveal how a psychotherapist helped him overcome these problems. If you read *Dibs,* try to analyze the causes of problems in adjustment with reference to Maslow's hierarchy of needs (i.e., in what way were the needs of safety, love and belongingness, and esteem frustrated?), and to relate the techniques of therapy to Carl Rogers's principles of nondirective therapy.

14–13   Examining Some "Basic Considerations for a Psychology of Personality"

In 1954 Gordon W. Allport delivered a series of lectures on personality at Yale University which the following year were published in book form under the title *Becoming* (subtitled "Basic Considerations for a Psychology of Personality"). Allport discusses the philosophical background of associationism and field theory and describes the difficulty of analyzing personality within an associationist framework. He proposes a simple yet penetrating theory of personality and touches on many factors which have been discussed in the text. Consequently, *Becoming* pulls together a number of the diverse ideas which you have been asked to examine, setting the stage for further thinking about aspects of psychology in general and personality in particular. If you peruse this short book, note points that seem especially meaningful and add your own reactions.

Techniques of Classroom Control

	Key Points
Classifications	Influence techniques: supporting self-control, giving situational assistance, fostering reality and value appraisal (Redl and Wattenberg)
Experiments and Studies	Positive effect of democratic leadership on boys, negative effect of autocratic leadership (Lippitt and White)
	Better response to integrative teachers than to dominating ones (Anderson)
	High self-esteem in children whose parents set definite limits (Coopersmith)
Concepts	Impact of classroom atmosphere on student behavior
	Causes of misbehavior: boredom; release of tension; desire for attention, recognition, and status
	Self-discipline (Neill)
Methodology	Taking into account common causes of misbehavior in establishing a constructive classroom atmosphere
	Using varied influence techniques to maintain constructive classroom control

Chapter Contents

Impact of Class Atmosphere
Dominative and Integrative Leadership

Classroom Control
Causes of Misbehavior
Suggestions for Maintaining Classroom Control

Establishing Self-control
Neill on Self-discipline
Values of Adult Control

Testing and Organizing Your Knowledge
of Key Points in Chapter 15

Experiments

1. Lippitt and White did a classic study in which groups of boys were exposed to different types of leadership. The results of this investigation may help you decide what kind of general class atmosphere you will attempt to establish when you begin to teach. In the following spaces describe the experimental design and the results of the Lippitt and White study, then comment on how you might take these findings into account in instituting and maintaining classroom control.

Experimental design and results of Lippitt and White study

_____

_____

_____

_____

_____

_____

How you might take results into account in establishing class atmosphere

_____

_____

_____

_____

_____

_____

2. H. H. Anderson compared the impact on students of teachers who were classified as *dominative* or *integrative*. In the spaces below describe the general conclusions he reached and comment on the implications of these findings.

Conclusions of Anderson study

_____

_____

_____

_____

_____

Implications for teachers

_____

_____

_____

_____

_____

3. Stanley Coopersmith carried out an extensive study of the factors that seemed to predispose a child to develop a high degree of self-esteem. In the spaces below note the general conclusions reached by Coopersmith and comment on how they might be related to the development of self-discipline.

Conclusions of Coopersmith study

_____

_____

_____

_____

How these conclusions relate to development of self-discipline

_____
_____
_____
_____
_____

Concepts

A. S. Neill bases the educational philosophy of Summerhill on a conception of "natural" self-discipline. While this approach seems to have many advantages, there are also limitations. In the spaces below briefly note what Neill regards as the advantages of a Summerhill approach, then comment on some possible disadvantages.

Advantages of a free approach to self-discipline

_____
_____
_____
_____
_____

Disadvantages of a free approach

_____
_____
_____
_____
_____

Methodology

1. In establishing and maintaining a classroom atmosphere which will permit a maximum amount of learning, you should be aware of common causes of misbehavior so that you can take steps to minimize or counteract them.

In the spaces below note two general guidelines for minimizing misbehavior due to boredom, tension, and desire for attention.

Boredom

a. _____

_____

b. _____

_____

Tension

a. _____

_____

b. _____

_____

Desire for attention

a. _____

_____

b. _____

_____

2. Despite your efforts to prevent misbehavior, some of your students will occasionally disrupt classroom activities. It will be simpler to handle such situations if you think ahead of time about specific techniques you can use when a problem erupts in class. Redl and Wattenberg have classified *influence techniques* into three major categories: supporting self-control, situational assistance, and reality and value appraisal. In the spaces below describe a specific technique illustrating a type of approach which falls within each subcategory listed.

Supporting self-control

Example of a *signal*

_____

_____

Example of *proximity control*

_____

_____

Situational assistance

Example of *support from routines*

_____

_____

Example of *nonpunitive exile*

_____

_____

Example of *removing seductive objects*

_____

_____

Reality and value appraisal

Example of a *direct appeal*

_____

_____

Example of *criticism and encouragement*

_____

_____

Example of *defining limits*

_____

_____

Suggestions for Further Reading,
Thinking, and Discussion

15–1   Analyzing Class Atmospheres You Have Experienced

The studies of Lippitt and White and of Anderson will seem more significant if you think about the different class atmospheres you have experienced. Look again at the descriptions of democratic, autocratic, and laissez-faire leaders (page 528 in the text) or those of dominative and integrative teachers (page 530 in the text) and recall a teacher who most closely exemplified each type. Then record your recollection of how you and your classmates reacted to the classroom atmosphere. Or compare the single class atmosphere you found most agreeable as a student with the one you found most disagreeable. Regardless of your approach, try to highlight the characteristics of the desirable and undesirable class "climates" and record the implications.

15–2   Sampling Friedenberg's Views on "Colonial Treatment" of Adolescents

In *Coming of Age in America* (1965) Edgar Z. Friedenberg argues that American "adolescents are among the last social groups in the world to be given the full nineteenth-century colonial treatment" (p. 4). Comparing youth workers to missionaries, he suggests that even in the better high schools of America teachers and administrators are primarily concerned with "control, distrust and punishment" (p. 36). He raises a basic question in the book: What does it cost in individual freedom and dignity to provide justice and equality in a mass society? If you are concerned about excessive control of young people, Friedenberg's analysis will interest you. Chapter 1 describes the general theme of the book. Chapter 2 gives his observations on what a typical American high school is like. (Compare your recollections of life in high school with the picture offered by Friedenberg.) In Chapter 3 he describes research he carried out in attempting to support his case. Chapter 4 includes a critique of teachers ("every high school student can be virtually certain that he will experience successive defeat at the hands of teachers with minds of really crushing banality" p. 181), and the final chapter concludes with prescriptions for reform (widespread use of programmed instruction and much more stringent selection of teachers). You might read one or more sections of *Coming of Age in America*. Summarize the arguments presented and note your own reactions.

15–3   Developing a Personal List of Dos and Don'ts for Classroom Control

The influence techniques described in Chapter 15 may be more meaningful if you analyze your own experiences with methods of classroom control. Think back to techniques you felt were excessively harsh or cruel. Were there incidents in which a teacher embarrassed or humiliated a child or caused considerable mental anguish? If so, describe the situation and then use it as a basis for drawing up a list of techniques to be avoided at all costs. You might also develop a set of procedures you definitely want to try.

15–4   Sampling Neill's Views on Discipline

In *Summerhill* (1960), A. S. Neill offers comments on the advantages of self-discipline. The sequence of topics in this book is a bit disorganized, but if you read "Self-Government" (page 45), "The Unfree Child" (page 95), "The Free Child" (page 104), "Obedience and Discipline" (page 155), and "Rewards and Punishments" (page 162), you will have a rather complete picture of Neill's views on how children should learn self-control. Whether you read any of the sections noted above or a different account of Neill's views on discipline, note the points that impress you the most and add your own reactions.

15–5   Reacting to Ginott's Suggestions on Discipline

Haim Ginott has written two best sellers on the subject of communication between parents and their offspring. *Between Parent and Child* (1965) will be of interest to you if you will be teaching at the elementary level. *Between Parent and Teenager* (1969) is more appropriate if you will be teaching at the secondary level. Both books describe how parents (and teachers) can make use of techniques similar to those developed by Carl Rogers in his nondirective therapy. There is considerable emphasis on assisting the child to understand his own feelings. Suggestions are offered on how praise and criticism can be expressed, and how to achieve a balance between permissiveness and limits as a basis for helping children develop responsibility, self-control, and independence. Not all of the methods described in these books can be used by teachers, and you may disagree with some of Ginott's recommendations, but as a general guide for establishing and maintaining classroom control his ideas can be quite helpful. If you read either book, list the points you think might be useful later.

15–6   Reading a More Complete Account of Classroom Control

For a more comprehensive analysis of common causes of behavior problems and suggestions on how to handle them, *Mental Hygiene in Teaching* (2nd ed., 1959) by Redl and Wattenberg is especially recommended. Chapter 10 is devoted to "Group Life in the Classroom," Chapter 11 to "The Psychological Roles of Teachers"; Chapter 13 presents a list of "Influence Techniques," and Chapter 14 notes "Some Common Dilemmas Teachers Face." Another excellent book on this subject (available as a paperback) is *Psychology in the Classroom* (2nd ed., 1968) by Rudolf Dreikurs. Part I deals with "Basic Principles," Part II with "Practical Applications." If you will be teaching at the secondary level and you want a down-to-earth list of dos and don'ts, you might browse through *The Teacher's Survival Guide* (1967) by Jenny Gray, subtitled "How to Teach Teen-agers and Live to Tell About It!" Blunt and breezy in style, the book is both entertaining and informative. If you sample one of these books, or a similar volume of your own choice, note ideas which strike you as potentially valuable.

16

Teaching for Your Own
Self-actualization

Key Points

Facts

Teacher dissatisfactions: large classes, too much nonacademic supervision, busywork, low salaries

Studies

Characteristics of effective teachers: generous in appraising others, happy in relating with students, well adjusted emotionally, preference for nondirective classroom methods (Ryans)

Problems of teachers: self-doubt, anxiety, sense of insecurity (Jersild)

Principles

Dependence of self-actualization on prior meeting of deficit needs (Maslow)

Two conflicting forces continually exerted on individual: one toward growth and health, another toward sickness and weakness (Maslow)

Self-knowledge as main road to self-improvement (Maslow)

Methodology

Dealing constructively with frustrations

Chapter Contents

Because the ideas discussed in Chapter 16 are intended to help you understand your own feelings about teaching, you are urged to sort out your thoughts in your own way. Accordingly, no section on testing and organizing your knowledge of Key Points is provided for this chapter.

Suggestions for Further Reading, Thinking, and Discussion

16–1 Analyzing the Goals You Hope to Achieve Through Teaching

Since you are considering devoting your professional life to teaching, you may wish to conduct a personal analysis of the goals you hope to achieve thereby. First list the factors which you feel led you to work toward a credential. What experiences predisposed you to choose teaching as a profession? What goals have you in mind? Then analyze these factors with respect to the needs for safety, belongingness, and esteem. From what you know about life in the schools, do you believe you will be able to satisfy your deficiency needs as a teacher? If you have wavered between teaching and a different kind of job, which alternative seems more likely to permit satisfaction of your needs for safety, belongingness, and esteem? If you have doubts about your feelings on teaching, self-analysis may help you resolve conflicts and uncertainties.

16–2 Estimating Your Abilities to Cope with the Frustrations of Teaching

A survey reported in the text lists common dissatisfactions noted by teachers. Frustrations arise from large classes, too much nonacademic supervision, excessive clerical busywork, and low salaries. In case you are wondering how completely committed you are to teaching, try to estimate how much these frustrations will irritate you. If you have seriously considered another sort of job as an alternative to teaching, you might interview one or two people who have chosen that line of endeavor and ask them what their major satisfactions and dissatisfactions are. Then compare their responses to those of teachers you know or to the lists of advantages and disadvantages of teaching noted in the text.

16–3   Trying to Gain Greater Understanding of Behavior Including Your Own

At the present time there is considerable interest in assisting individuals to understand their own behavior better. Humanistic psychology, the discovery approach, the perceptual view of behavior, nondirective therapy, and sensitivity training—not to mention the desire of college students for education which has personal relevance—are all manifestations of this trend. Basic to the concern for self-knowledge is the belief that only when a person understands his own behavior can he understand the behavior of others. If you have a general interest in self-understanding and/or feel that you may be better able to comprehend your students' behavior by becoming more aware of your own behavior, explore the dynamics of adjustment. Courses on this subject are offered in the psychology departments of many colleges. Encounter groups conducted by reputable and experienced leaders provide another semiformal framework for developing self-understanding. In the absence of structured situations, or if you prefer to think things through on your own, read one or more books intended to foster understanding of behavior. You might choose from the following: *In Search of Self* (1952) by Arthur Jersild, *The Art of Growing* (1962) by Robert E. Nixon, *The Transparent Self* (1964) by Sidney M. Jourard, *Lives in Progress* (2nd ed., 1966) by Robert W. White, *Toward a Psychology of Being* (2nd ed., 1968) by Abraham H. Maslow, or *Man's Search for Himself* (1950) and *Love and Will* (1969) by Rollo May.

Answers to Statistics Questions 4 and 5 in Chapter 11

Frequency Distribution

Score Tally X	Frequency f	Product of score and frequency fX
47 /	1	47
46 /	1	46
45 /	1	45
44 /	1	44
43 /	1	43
42 /	1	42
41 /	1	41
40 ///	3	120
39 ///	3	117
38 ///	3	114
37 //	2	74
36		
35 /	1	35
34 /	1	34
33 /	1	33
32 //	2	64
31		
30 /	1	30
29 /	1	29
	N = 25	ΣfX = 958

Calculation of Mean:

$$\text{Mean (M)} = \frac{\text{Sum total of scores } (\Sigma fX)}{\text{Number of scores (N)}} = \frac{958}{25} = 38.32$$

Calculation of Median:

$$\text{Median} = \text{Number of scores } \frac{(N) + 1}{2} = \frac{25 + 1}{2} = 13$$

Count from top or bottom until 13th tally is reached = 39

Bibliography

Allport, Gordon W., 1955. *Becoming.* New Haven, Conn.: Yale University Press.

Almy, Millie C., E. Chittenden, and P. Miller, 1966. *Young Children's Thinking.* New York: Teachers College, Columbia University.

Bair, Medill, and Richard G. Woodward, 1964. *Team Teaching in Action.* Boston: Houghton Mifflin.

Barzun, Jacques, 1944. *Teacher in America.* New York: Doubleday.

Barzun, Jacques, 1959. *The House of Intellect.* New York: Harper.

Barzun, Jacques, 1968. *The American University: How It Runs, Where It is Going.* New York: Harper & Row.

Bernstein, Emmanuel, 1968. "What Does a Summerhill Old School Tie Look Like?" *Psychology Today,* 2 (5): 37–70.

Bloom, Benjamin S. (ed.), 1956. *Taxonomy of Educational Objectives. Handbook I: Cognitive Domain.* New York: McKay.

Bloom, Benjamin S., 1964. *Stability and Change in Human Characteristics.* New York: Wiley.

Boring, Edwin G., 1950. *A History of Experimental Psychology,* 2nd ed. New York: Appleton-Century-Crofts.

Boring, Edwin G., and Gardner Lindzey (eds.), 1967. *A History of Psychology in Autobiography,* Vol. IV. New York: Appleton-Century-Crofts.

Braithwaite, Edward R., 1959. *To Sir with Love.* Englewood Cliffs, N.J.: Prentice-Hall.

Brownell, John A., and Harris A. Taylor, 1962. "Theoretical Perspectives for Teaching Teams," *Phi Delta Kappan,* 43:150–157.

Bruner, Jerome S., 1960. *The Process of Education.* New York: Vintage Books.

Bruner, Jerome S., 1966. *Toward a Theory of Instruction.* Cambridge, Mass.: Belknap Press of Harvard University Press.

Callahan, Raymond E., 1962. *Education and the Cult of Efficiency.* Chicago: University of Chicago Press.

Chauncey, Henry, and John E. Dobbin, 1963. *Testing: Its Place in Education Today.* New York: Harper & Row.

Coleman, James S., 1966. *Equality of Educational Opportunity*. Washington: U.S. Department of Health, Education, and Welfare, Office of Education.

Combs, Arthur W., and Donald Snygg, 1959. *Individual Behavior,* rev. ed. New York: Harper.

DeHaan, Robert F., and Jack Kough, 1956. *Helping Children with Special Needs.* Chicago: Science Research Associates.

Dreikurs, Rudolf, 1968. *Psychology in the Classroom,* 2nd ed. New York: Harper & Row.

Dunn, Lloyd M. (ed.), 1963. *Exceptional Children in the Schools.* New York: Holt, Rinehart and Winston.

Ebel, Robert L., 1965. *Measuring Educational Achievement.* Englewood Cliffs, N.J.: Prentice-Hall.

Ellis, Henry, 1965. *The Transfer of Learning.* New York: Macmillan.

Environment, Heredity, and Intelligence, 1970. Reprint Series No. 2. Cambridge, Mass.: *Harvard Educational Review.*

Erickson, Marion, 1965. *The Mentally Retarded Child in the Classroom.* New York: Macmillan.

Erikson, Erik H., 1958. *Young Man Luther.* New York: Norton.

Erikson, Erik H., 1968. *Identity: Youth and Crisis.* New York: Norton.

Erikson, Erik H., 1969. *Gandhi's Truth.* New York: Norton.

Evans, Richard I., 1968. *B. F. Skinner: The Man and His Ideas.* New York: Dutton.

Flavell, John H., 1963. *The Developmental Psychology of Jean Piaget.* Princeton, N.J.: Van Nostrand.

Fliegler, Louis A. (ed.), 1961. *Curriculum Planning for the Gifted.* Englewood Cliffs, N.J.: Prentice-Hall.

Frankel, Charles, 1968. *Education and the Barricades.* New York: Norton.

Friedenberg, Edgar Z., 1959. *The Vanishing Adolescent.* New York: Dell.

Friedenberg, Edgar Z., 1965. *Coming of Age in America.* New York: Random House.

Frost, Joe L., and Glenn R. Hawkes (eds.), 1970. *The Disadvantaged Child: Issues and Innovations,* 2nd ed. Boston: Houghton Mifflin.

Gagné, Robert M., 1965. *The Conditions of Learning.* New York: Holt, Rinehart and Winston.

Gallagher, James J., 1964. *Teaching the Gifted Child.* Boston: Allyn & Bacon.

Gardner, John W., 1961. *Excellence.* New York: Harper & Row.

Gardner, John W., 1965. *Self-Renewal.* New York: Harper & Row.

Gardner, John W., 1968. *No Easy Victories.* New York: Harper & Row.

Ginott, Haim, 1965. *Between Parent and Child.* New York: Avon Books.

Ginott, Haim, 1969. *Between Parent and Teen-ager.* New York: Macmillan.

Ginsburg, Herbert, and Sylvia Opper, 1969. *Piaget's Theory of Intellectual Development: An Introduction.* Englewood Cliffs, N.J.: Prentice-Hall.

Glasser, William, 1969. *Schools without Failure.* New York: Harper & Row.

Goertzel, Victor, and Mildred Goertzel, 1962. *Cradles of Eminence.* Boston: Little, Brown.

Goodman, Paul, 1956. *Growing Up Absurd.* New York: Vintage Books.

Goodman, Paul, 1964. *Compulsory Miseducation.* New York: Horizon Press.

Gray, Jenny, 1967. *The Teacher's Survival Guide.* Palo Alto, Calif.: Fearon.

Havighurst, Robert, 1952. *Developmental Tasks and Education.* New York: Longmans, Green.

Havighurst, Robert, 1953. *Human Development and Education.* New York: Longmans, Green.

Herndon, James, 1968. *The Way it Spozed to Be.* New York: Simon and Schuster.

Hersey, John, 1960. *The Child Buyer.* New York: Knopf.

Highet, Gilbert, 1957. *The Art of Teaching.* New York: Vintage Books.

Hoffmann, Banesh, 1962. *The Tyranny of Testing.* New York: Crowell-Collier.

Holt, John, 1964. *How Children Fail.* New York: Pitman.

Holt, John, 1967. *How Children Learn.* New York: Pitman.

Holt, John, 1969. *The Underachieving School.* New York: Pitman.

Hunt, James McV., 1961. *Intelligence and Experience.* New York: Ronald Press.

Huxley, Aldous, 1932. *Brave New World.* New York: Harper.

Huxley, Aldous, 1958. *Brave New World Revisited.* New York: Harper.

Huxley, Aldous, 1962. *Island.* New York: Harper & Row.

Ilg, Frances, and Louise Bates Ames, 1955. *The Gesell Institute's Child Behavior.* New York: Dell.

Ilg, Frances, and Louise Bates Ames, 1965. *School Readiness.* New York: Harper & Row.

Itard, Jean Marc, 1962. *The Wild Boy of Aveyron.* New York: Appleton-Century-Crofts.

Jensen, Arthur R., 1969. "How Much Can We Boost I.Q. and Scholastic Achievement?" *Harvard Educational Review,* 39, Winter.

Jersild, Arthur, 1952. *In Search of Self.* New York: Teachers College, Columbia University.

Jones, Richard M., 1968. *Fantasy and Feeling in Education.* New York: New York University Press.

Jourard, Sidney M., 1964. *The Transparent Self.* Princeton, N.J.: Van Nostrand.

Kaufman, Bel, 1964.   *Up the Down Staircase.*   New York: Avon Books.

Kohl, Herbert, 1967.   *36 Children.*   New York: New American Library.

Kozol, Jonathan, 1967.   *Death at an Early Age.*   Boston: Houghton Mifflin.

Leonard, George, 1969.   *Education and Ecstasy.*   New York: Dell.

Lewis, W. Arthur, 1969.   "The Road to the Top Is through Higher Education— Not Black Studies," *New York Times Magazine,* May 11, pp. 34–54.

Linkletter, Art, 1962.   *Kids Sure Rite Funny.*   New York: Crest Books.

Linkletter, Art, 1965.   *A Child's Garden of Misinformation.*   New York: Crest Books.

Lorenz, Konrad, 1952.   *King Solomon's Ring.*   New York: Thomas Y. Crowell.

Lorenz, Konrad, 1966.   *On Aggression.*   New York: Harcourt, Brace and World.

Lysaught, Jerome P., and Clarence M. Williams, 1963.   *A Guide to Programed Instruction.*   New York: Wiley.

Mager, Robert F., 1962.   *Preparing Instructional Objectives.*   Palo Alto, Calif.: Fearon.

Mager, Robert F., 1968.   *Developing Attitude toward Learning.*   Palo Alto, Calif.: Fearon.

Mager, Robert F., and Kenneth M. Beach, Jr., 1967.   *Developing Vocational Instruction.*   Palo Alto, Calif.: Fearon.

Markle, Susan Meyer, 1964.   *Good Frames and Bad: A Grammar of Frame Writing.*   New York: Wiley.

Maslow, Abraham H., 1968.   *Toward a Psychology of Being,* 2nd ed.   Princeton, N.J.: Van Nostrand.

May, Rollo, 1950.   *Man's Search for Himself.*   New York: Norton.

May, Rollo, 1969.   *Love and Will.*   New York: Norton.

Montessori, Maria, 1964.   *The Montessori Method.*   New York: Schocken Books.

Montessori, Maria, 1965.   *Dr. Montessori's Own Handbook.*   New York: Schocken Books.

Montessori, Maria, 1966.   *Spontaneous Activity in Education.*   New York: Schocken Books.

Murchison, Carl (ed.), 1932.   *A History of Psychology in Autobiography,* Vol. II. New York: Russell & Russell.

Murray, Henry A., and Clyde Kluckhohn, 1948.   *Personality in Nature, Society and Culture.*   New York: Knopf.

Mussen, Paul H., Jonas Langer, and Martin Covington (eds.), 1969.   *Trends and Issues in Developmental Psychology.*   New York: Holt, Rinehart and Winston.

Neill, A. S., 1960.   *Summerhill.*   New York: Hart.

Nixon, Robert E., 1962.   *The Art of Growing.*   New York: Random House.

Ornstein, Allan C., and Philip D. Vairo, 1969.   *How to Teach Disadvantaged Youth.*   New York: McKay.

Passow, Harry A. (ed.), 1962. *Education in Depressed Areas.* New York: Teachers College, Columbia University.

Peddiwell, J. Abner, 1939. *The Saber-Tooth Curriculum.* New York: McGraw-Hill.

Pipe, Peter, 1966. *Practical Programming.* New York: Holt, Rinehart and Winston.

Polya, Gyorgy, 1954. *How to Solve It.* Princeton, N.J.: Princeton University Press.

Postman, Neil, and Charles Weingartner, 1969. *Teaching as a Subversive Activity.* New York: Delacorte Press.

Redl, Fritz, and William M. Wattenberg, 1959. *Mental Hygiene in Teaching,* 2nd ed. New York: Harcourt, Brace and World.

Report of the National Advisory Commission on Civil Disorders, 1968. New York: Bantam Books.

Robinson, Halbert B., and Nancy M. Robinson, 1965. *The Mentally Retarded Child.* New York: McGraw-Hill.

Rogers, Carl R., 1961. *On Becoming a Person.* Boston: Houghton Mifflin.

Rogers, Carl R., 1963. "Learning to Be Free," in S. Farber and R. Wilson (eds.), *Conflict and Creativity: Control of the Mind.* New York: McGraw-Hill.

Rogers, Carl, and Barry Stevens, 1967. *Person to Person: The Problem of Being Human.* Lafayette, Calif.: Real People Press.

Rosenthal, Robert, and Lenore Jacobson, 1968. *Pygmalion in the Classroom.* New York: Holt, Rinehart and Winston.

Ross, Leonard Q., 1937. *The Education of H*Y*M*A*N K*A*P*L*A*N.* New York: Harper.

Rosten, Leo, 1959. *The Return of H*Y*M*A*N K*A*P*L*A*N.* New York: Harper.

Sanders, Norris M., 1966. *Classroom Questions:What Kinds?* New York: Harper & Row.

Seagoe, May V., 1961. *A Teacher's Guide to the Learning Process,* 2nd ed. Dubuque, Iowa: Brown.

Sellar, W. C., and R. J. Yeatman, 1931. *1066 and All That.* New York: Dutton.

Sexton, Patricia, 1969. *The Feminized Male.* New York: Random House.

Sexton, Patricia, 1970. "How the American Boy Is Feminized," *Psychology Today,* 3 (8): 23–67.

Shaffer, Laurence, and Edward Shoben, Jr., 1956. *The Psychology of Adjustment,* 2nd ed. Boston: Houghton Mifflin.

Shulman, Lee S., and Evan R. Keislar (eds.), 1966. *Learning by Discovery.* Chicago: Rand McNally.

Skinner, B. F., 1948. *Walden Two.* New York: Macmillan.

Skinner, B. F., 1953. *Science and Human Behavior.* New York: Macmillan.

Skinner, B. F., 1959. "A Case History in Scientific Method," in Sigmund Koch (ed.), *Psychology: A Study of Science.* New York: McGraw-Hill.

Skinner, B. F., 1968. *The Technology of Teaching.* New York: Appleton-Century-Crofts.

Smith, H. Allen, 1956. *Write Me a Poem, Baby.* Boston: Little, Brown.

Smith, H. Allen, 1959. *Don't Get Perconel with a Chicken.* Boston: Little, Brown.

Snitzer, Herb, 1968. *Living at Summerhill.* New York: Collier Books.

Stephens, J. M., 1967. *The Process of Schooling.* New York: Holt, Rinehart and Winston.

Suchman, J. Richard, 1961. "Inquiry Training: Building Skills for Autonomous Discovery," *Merrill-Palmer Quarterly,* 7 (3): 147–171.

Suchman, J. Richard, 1963. *The Elementary School Training Program in Scientific Inquiry.* Urbana: University of Illinois Press.

Thelen, Herbert A., 1960. *Education and the Human Quest.* New York: Wiley.

Thelen, Herbert A., 1967. *Classroom Grouping for Teachability.* New York: Wiley.

Torrance, Ellis Paul, 1962a. "Developing Creative Thinking through School Experiences," in S. Parnes and G. Harding (eds.), *A Source Book for Creative Thinking.* New York: Scribner.

Torrance, Ellis Paul, 1962b. *Guiding Creative Talent.* Englewood Cliffs, N.J.: Prentice-Hall.

Torrance, Ellis Paul, 1965. *Gifted Children in the Classroom.* New York: Macmillan.

Webster, Staten W. (ed.), 1966. *The Disadvantaged Learner.* San Francisco: Chandler.

White, Robert W., 1966. *Lives in Progress,* 2nd ed. New York: Holt, Rinehart and Winston.

Whyte, William H., Jr., 1956. *The Organization Man.* Garden City, N.Y.: Doubleday.

Woodring, Paul, 1953. *Let's Talk Sense about Our Schools.* New York: McGraw-Hill.

Woodring, Paul, 1957. *A Fourth of a Nation.* New York: McGraw-Hill.

Woodring, Paul, 1968. *The Higher Learning in America: A Reassessment.* New York: McGraw-Hill.

Young, Michael, 1959. *The Rise of the Meritocracy.* New York: Random House.

Notes

Notes

Notes

Notes

Notes

Notes

CDEFGHIJ— H —7654321